The Suicide Attacker
Nightmare of the Century

by Shkelzen Marevci

RoseDog ♣ Books

PITTSBURGH, PENNSYLVANIA 15238

RoseDog Books
585 Alpha Drive
Pittsburgh, PA 15238
Visit our website at www.rosedogbookstore.com

ISBN: 978-1-4809-8350-2
eISBN: 978-1-4809-8327-4

Note: The look of a person (whether he is wearing a beard, or any different kind of head cover, as well as the way he is dressing), while practicing different forms of certain religious rituals, doesn't necessarily make him neither a more peaceful person nor a more violent one.

Part 1

Chapter 1

With his insistence, we decided to pay a visit to our uncle in Belgium. To tell the truth, we didn't have the luxury to travel abroad at that time, because our family revenues were limited. Our father died when my sister, Besa, and I were at a very young age, so since then the burden of our family's responsibility laid on my mother's shoulder. Facing courageously all the difficulties, my mother managed to fulfill all our family needs. We provided enough money for food, clothes, and education from her salary as a teacher and her profits from creating bridal accessories, a craft that she had learned from her aunt. Thanks to her hard work and her wisdom, we menaged to cope with those difficult times successfully. However, that money wasn't enough to travel to other countries, let alone to countries like Belgium, where the living was so expensive and still is. My uncle offered to pay all the expenses for the trip, but my mother wasn't so keen to accept his offer, because she didn't want to become a burden for our uncle, although he was in fine economic conditions. Her pride would not allow her take advantage of others, let alone of her own brother. When finally she accepted, Besa and I were very happy, not to say that it seemed to us almost unbelievable. Our father's absence in our life on one side, and our mother's sacrifice while striving to fulfill our needs on the other, had made us shy to express our desires, so although we were eager to go there, it was my mother who sealed this decision making.

We booked the plane tickets a week before our departure. Being excited, Besa and I asked our mother to prepare our luggage right after that, but she told us that we could make ready only a day before the trip. She was cooling our hilarity with her prudency. When the great day came, we went to the airport and I couldn't wait to step on the plane. For Besa and me it was our first time time ever, although my mother had travelled together with my father when he was alive - They had were happy together, but since fate decided, my father left her a widow when she was a young woman. - So, we passed the check in. Besa got anxious because of flying. Her face had become pale. I kept joking with her, while she kept looking at me speechless. She had nausea, so she wanted to go to the restroom before we stepped on the plane. Her condition was ruining somehow the magic of the trip, so I prayed that it ended there…

When we finally took our seats, I kept an eye on Besa while she kept closing her eyes in a titanic effort to sleep. Hoping she would calm down, I was watching the view outside the plane window. It was amazing - at the same time, a real pleasure - the fact that a metallic transport mean with almost a hundred passengers on its board was flying in the open blue skies, without even vibrating the coffee in our cups, while giant cotton flocks of clouds were floating beneath us. Indeed, it was amazing how the Omnipotent and the Knower, while giving the human being mind and logic to cope with his life, gave him also the possibility to build such a transport mean to fly around the world with such a speed, thus making easer his own life. My first flight, what a breathtaking and unforgettable experience in the horizons of the blue skies! I couldn't hide my joy and excitement. My face showed it on its every inch. My happy smile was mirrored on my mother's face every time she looked at me. But her face expression used to change completely every time she looked at my sister's pale and scared face. As it happens to every mother, her children's feelings and wellbeing were more important to her than hers.

In the meantime, the stewardess made the announcement to land, so we had to fasten our seatbelts. We paid attention to the stewardess' suggestions and took the necessary measures to land safely. At the passport control desk I was impressed by the attitude of the Belgium Border Police. They proceeded politely, with a smile in their face. Finally, we took our hold luggages and followed the exit signs until we saw my uncle together with his daughter Fiona, who was the same age as Besa. My uncle welcomed us and we hugged each-other cordially. We left the airport terminal and we went toward the parking lot where my uncle had parked his car. We were almost flying from joy and my uncle was joking and making us laugh. Even Besa recovered. We were all so happy as people are usually when they meet with their beloved ones after a long time of absence... When suddenly there was an apocalyptic explosion. It felt like the Earth was torn apart. We were petrified. All of a sudden, all of us four turned around at the same time as if by a remote control. Then, for four or five seconds we would look at each-other and then again at the direction from where the explosion came. People began to run like a disoriented colony of ants. Nobody could understand a thing. We looked around bewildered. A man ran out of the terminal with a 5-6 year old child, covered in blood, with his child's head and arm waving, like they were detached from the body pending under the skin. A man, with his arms and legs covered in blood ran 10-15 meters out of the terminal and couldn't make it further, but lost consciousness and threw himself onto the floor. Other people flocked out of the terminal screaming and crying. Another child, with his forehead soaking in blood, was looking around for his parents. A young man was running as fast as he could, together with an elderly woman, away from the terminal, but in vain, because it seemed that the woman's bowls were almost falling out of her belly. With one hand on the boy's shoulder and the other she kept her belly bleeding unceasingly. A man and a woman were screaming scarily:

'Please, help us!' while running by the ruins of a wall that had collapsed because of the explosion.

Their daughter was lying under the ruins. They cried and prayed in a way that in other circumstances they would have moved everyone's hearts, but in that very moment nobody could help them, because they were trying to save themselves. The first to come to rescue were the firefighters. Then the paramedics assisted the wounded that were outside the terminal, because they couldn't enter inside the terminal without the permission of the Security Forces. The couple, who didn't know whether their daughter was still alive under the ruins, was imploring to the paramedics to go to her rescue. But the paramedics couldn't do anything without further orders. A bit later two other explosions shook the earth. Security Forces flocked in. We didn't know what exactly had happened. We were shocked and felt destroyed about what we saw, that maybe it was five per cent of what had happened inside. Fjona and I had nausea. Finally, my uncle got hold of himself and told my mother:

'Let's get out of here, sister!'

Because of shock, my uncle couldn't remember where he had parked his car. We wandered a bit around the parking lot until we finally found it and took off immediately. Besa and Fjona were feeling nauseous. My uncle had to stop his car, but Besa vomited inboard. Only Fjona made it to get out of the car. The rest of us were thunderstruck and our limbs were numb, unable to help. Following our destination, my uncle would slap his head, saying:

'Curse on you for your filthy deeds!'

I couldn't understand who he was speaking about. Meanwhile, confused and bewildered, my mother kept looking into the void, thanking God that we were safe and sound. Her face was pale. My uncle's house wasn't far from the airport, but it took us almost one hour to reach there because of the chaos in the traffic by the fire engines, ambulances, police cars, added to the normal traffic. When my uncle's wife opened the door, she looked at us like she had in front of her a bunch of phantoms. In fact, she had felt her apartment trembling a few times, but the noise in the kitchen had prevented her from hearing the noise of the blasts. Besides, she was too busy to watch television.

'Water, water! Give water to the children' my uncle told her.

She went to the kitchen and rushed back with a glass in one hand and a water jug in the other, asking:

'O my God! What happened?'

My uncle lied down on the sofa and stayed speechless and motionless, resembling to a dead person. Then, he began to repeat the same phrase:

'The terrorists, the terrorists… For sure it was a terrorist attack. Turn on the TV to see what happened!' he told to his wife.

The warmth of my uncle's house made us feel better. We gradually began to get hold of ourselves and turned our attention on TV in an effort to understand what had happened. On the breaking news was being reported about a suspected terrorist attack, with thirty five deadly victims, among them three under the age of ten, and seventy two injured, among them eight kids in serious conditions. The number of casualties was increasing. Something was sure, except the terrorists that exploded themselves all the other victims were innocent people.

A few days had passed but we still were shocked. We kept thanking God. Indeed, we escaped that slaughter miraculously. My uncle sent us to visit the most interesting and the most famous places in Brussels. But despite all his efforts to entertain us I myself couldn't get rid of the thought about that day. The death toll had reached one hundred and seventy, while the number of the injured was two hundred and thirty four. Why that horrible slaughter in the name of religion? My mother used to pray five times every day, and she used to read book about religion and tell us about the message of peace, laudable moral virtues, social harmony, tolerance between religions, that religion spread, all in all to have a safe society. What we witnessed that day had nothing to do with the religion we knew. I couldn't find a reason that would justify that horrendous act.

After a month in Brussels we had to go home. My uncle insisted to send us to Kosovo himself by car, because he feared any other tragedy. It was e very long itinerary, almost 20 000 kilometers trip, but he was firm in his decision. Even my mother couldn't dissuade him. Although I had a good time during my stay in Brussels, the images of that gloomy day were haunting me. I had to take tranquilizers. The trip was tiresome. We finally arrived home exhausted after a 34 hours drive.

Chapter 2

In my life I had never practiced any religious rituals. In my family we were not religious, except my mother. However I felt connected to the religious principles because of the fact that we lived a family life full of harmony, and we loved and respected each-other, in accordance with the religious teachings. In other words, we lived a life of dignity. Regarding my mother, she tried hard to compensate the absence of our father's love. Thanks to her efforts and our diligence as children we became a good example at our school and in our neighborhood. At a young age, I used to meditate about God, about His creation of the Universe and life that were clear signs of His existence. I was in a dilemma why we couldn't see Him, but after thinking and analyzing deeply I would deduct that it was sufficient to contemplate on the evident traces of His divine work. The terrorist act in Brussels, which had touched us deeply, made me think why such an act aims to take revenge against only innocent people. I began to ask seriously for an answer. I was 18 years old at that time. I could barely sleep because of the shock, so meditating and sleeping became my best friends at night.

One night, I was reading a book on the terrace of my house, sipping the coffee that now on I used to drink during my reading. I was lost in the reading so the coffee got cold. I thought to refill the cup with hot coffee. In a try to stand, I raised my head in the endless night sky, adorned by myriads and myriads of stars. I felt my body shaking from tip to toe. A voice inside me told me to leave the past behind me and to think about the moment I was living. Observing the Moon and the stars I began to meditate about the creation of the Universe and its creation in a perfect order:

'How is it created in such a perfect order? How is it possible that those giant stars are created in such an endless number, impossible to be counted? What about the Sun? Who or what makes it to stay in the same "place" through millions of years? How is it possible that the Earth rotates around its axle and around the Sun at such vertiginous speed, in the meantime it doesn't change its trajectory otherwise it would crush to another giant cosmic object?'

The precisely coordinated movements of the celestial bodies of all forms and sizes wandering seemingly in an unspecified destination made me wonder why the Sun and the Earth couldn't move randomly. Are these two obeying anybody's order? If so, by obeying this order the skies and the Earth where we, the human beings, lived was put in order by Creator of the Universe. In the meantime, I felt my breathing had become heavy. I thought:

'O Lord, how is it possible that we breathe the exact amount of the oxygen from the air so we can live normally on this Earth?'

And yet, asking myself more astonished:

'Would it still be possible life on Earth, if the amount of the oxygen in the air increased, exceeding the limits?'

And yet again:

'What if, instead, the same amount of oxygen decreased…?'

While I was wiping my sweat from my forefront, this act reminded me the key element of life, water. I thought:

'What about the rain that supports life on Earth? Indeed if it fell all at once it would be apocalyptic for us. Then who made the rain fall drops by drops in order to support life and not to destroy it?'

Then I looked around, in an effort to explore the micro-cosmos around me. I grabbed some soil from a plant pot. That reminded me the seeds planted on earth, irrigated by rain and snow water, blessed by the Sun rays, helped in growing and sprouting plants on the surface. Instinctively I grabbed the cup of coffee but it slipped off my hand and broke on the terrace floor. That reminded me that the random happenings don't create things, they destroy them. How much time was needed to make the cup that in an instant lost its form and function by being broken randomly in an instant! And to think, how much time, effort and knowledge are spent to make and discover things in order to support and facilitate people's life! Isn't the order in the Universe a message from God that we must try to establish order and peace on Earth and not anarchy and violence?

Midnight had long passed and I was lost in my meditation. Suddenly I felt a hand tapping on my shoulder. It was my beloved mother's, but I got scared for an instant. She noticed it and held me in her arms tightly. I felt my mother's love in every inch of my body:

'I am sorry, my beloved son! I didn't mean to scare you.'

She didn't tell me that I woke her up with the noise I had made breaking the cup while almost everything and soul had fallen asleep. I kissed her in her forefront and her hands, telling her nothing had happened.

'Why aren't you sleeping?' She asked me.

'What time is it?' I asked her, instead of answering.

'It is 2:00 o'clock,' my mother answered.

I couldn't believe my ears. I thought it was still midnight. I took my mother and we went in our bedrooms, but I had to struggle with my bed until I finally slept.

Chapter 3

Days went by, but I couldn't find my inner peace. There were two thoughts fighting against each-other: the first one, justifying those evil actions as imposed by given circumstances; the second thought was categorically against. I needed to confirm that who killed in the name of religion was totally wrong. I didn't know any professional to talk to about my situation. I had accumulated psychological problems. I could barely sleep and when I finally could sleep I had nightmares. Besa had more or less the same problems. She used to wake up in the middle of the night crying. Only my mother seemed to have dealt properly with the trauma. Anyhow I had doubts about that. She hid her worries so not to multiple ours. After all, a mother is like a burning candle that burns herself to spread light sacrificing herself for her children's sake.

One morning, while we were eating breakfast, my mother told us with an angry voice:

'I won't tolerate anymore your anxiety and your post traumatic stress. You need to get hold of yourselves. Enough is enough! We are going to visit a psychologist, today.'

We begged her not to visit any psychologist. We were obsessed with the idea that who visited a mental health counselor in fact was mentally ill. But no! It's not true that only a mentally ill person would go to visit a psychologist. My mother tried to explain us that a mental counselor dealt also with everyday emotional problems, such as the stress caused in school, work, family, as well as different anxieties, phobias etc.

'Mom, please don't send us to the doctor,' implored her Besa.

I wanted to speak too, but the expression on my mother's face told me it would be useless.

'Besa, my sweetheart, we must get rid of this psychological complex. Prejudices are preventing us to get cured from the symptoms of stress and phobias that are otherwise easily cured. You aren't aware of your crying and screaming in your sleep. Besides, it's been ever since, Beni is barely sleeping. Your dreams have a strong meaning. Today we will go to visit the psychologist, because you have posttraumatic stress. You will see you will get relieved. I can't bear to see you in these conditions anymore.'

In the end we gave up. My mother felt remorse that she tolerated the situation up to this point. She was categorical. I felt mercy for my mother, because I knew she was trying to do this for our best.

'No problem, mom,' I said to her. 'We will do as you please.'

Besa kept frowning, with her head down, but my mother worry was more important:

'Besa, we must understand our mother. She is doing this for our sake. We must obey her because she knows best. Calm down and raise your head, please! I am sure the visit to the doctor will help us,' I said to my sister.

Besa stood up and approached our mother. She kissed her on her forehead and squeezed her head over her chest in sign of acceptance:

'As you please, mom,' she said to her.

Chapter 4

That morning I woke up lazily. I had indeed a good sleep. After a month since the first session by the psychologist I was improving day by day, so I kept thanking my mother for taking that decisive step. Finally, Besa and I were relieved enormously of our symptoms and were trying to go back to normal life. However, the questions raised inside me were still there. It wasn't the psychologist that had the answers. Instead, I should read books and discuss with the right people about the dilemma that were corroding my inner self: 'How was it possible to kill, mutilate and terrorize innocent people in the name of a so called religious cause?' It was absolutely unacceptable. That same morning, I met Agim, a friend of mine, and we went together to the coffee bar where we usually used to go to drink the morning coffee. There, Gazi, another friend of us, was waiting for us together with Adnan. Gazi used to take care of Adnan, because he was born paralysed and needed perpetually help, and Gazi had been helping him unconditionally since he was a young child. Even when we used to play, he would bring Adnan to watch us playing. Judging by Gazi's carefulness toward him anyone would say he was his brother.

I began to talk to them about the serious issues that were troubling me. In fact, we were not so religious. I used to go to the mosque only for the Friday prayers, but my friends didn't step foot on the mosque at all. Thus, we started a heated debate. Adnan was very intelligent and used to make very interesting points, but he was not always right. On the other hand, Gazi preferred listening over speaking, but his word was like a seal to any discussion and he was firm in his decision makings. As for me, I was a curious boy. I wanted to know everything useful that happened around me. Often my friends would tease. To them I was the most curious boy in the world, as a consequence, the most unbearable and boring one. To tell the truth, the four of us made a distinguished group, dealing successfully with topics higher in level then our age.

In the end, we decided to go to attend the Friday prayers. iT was on Wednesday. No one of us refused. Adnan was being shy, because he knew without our assistance he couldn't go to the mosque. He was powerless and helpless at the same time. Gazi petted him on his chest saying to him:

'Adnan, my best friend, as long as I am around, you will be part of everything we do. You will be wherever I am.'

Adnan smiled, nodding, and his dimples crinkled up over his face. He was an intelligent and a discreet boy, and of course such situations embarrassed him, because he felt as if he were a burden to us although we didn't feel like that at all, especially Gazi.

Chapter 5

'It is out of question. It will be only me and no one else. You Gimi keep the wheelchair and you Beni help us!"

Agim was opening Gazi's wheelchair, while Gazi and me took him from his brother's car to sit him on the wheelchair. Gazi pushed the wheelchair to the front door to the mosque after us. Before we entered the mosque, Gazi cleaned the wheelchair wheels with a piece of cloth. The mosque was half full. All the men waiting there greeted Adnan and Gazi. We took place somewhere convenient. The people were flowing into the mosque. After fifteen minutes, the Imam came. He put on the microphone and greeted us with a *Salam alaykum*. After a while, the Mu'adhin called the Adhan. The men sat in straight rows after the Imam, some of them closing the Kur'an they were reading, some others leaving aside the religious books they were holding. The Imam stepped up in the Minbar and after saying some prayers in Arabic, he began his preaching:

'Dear Muslim brothers, today in this day of Friday, in front of you, from this Minbar, I want to address you my concerns about the serious situation in the today Islamic world. Some people while they have read only some religious books they think they know religion in that higher level that can give religious interpretations and judgments. The most dangerous think is that the incompetent voice mutes the competent voice. Imagine economists speak up about medicine instead of doctors. Or worse, imagine ignorant people speak up about medical issues. Sincerely, the deviation of the Islamic teachings up to this degree is hurtful, so I advise you with the highest love and sincerity not to fall prey of liars and the manipulators that speak in the name of the Islam. This will aggravate the situation and endanger our youth regarding the Islamic teachings. Dear youth, I am well aware about the strong emotions that the religion brings, but beware of any manipulation. Evil people and ignorant religious people insist to deviate you from the right path. They might do it because of their ignorance or because of they want to do evil or even because of personal purposes. Once again, I advise you to protect yourselves and your families, because we will be accountable in the Day of the Judgment for all the deeds that we had to do but we didn't do and the deeds we were forbidden to do but we did them anyway.'

After Imam's word, we prayed. I knew how to pray but my friends no. Gazi, Adnan and Agim followed my movements. After we finished the prayer we wished each-other for an accepted prayer by God. We waited until all the men went out otherwise it would be possible to push Gazi's wheelchair through the crowd.

We were all happy, especially Gazi and Adnan. Adnan was smiling as joyfully as I had never seen his dimples crinkled up so deeply over his face. It was his first prayer. Gazi also was saying that he had a special feeling he never had before. Agim and me could understand them, though I felt it more often because I had stepped up in the mosque ever since.

We used to pray every Friday. We went from another mosque to another, and we even frequented other mosques in other cities. One day Gazi told us that it was an improvised mosque, maybe in the basement of an apartment building, in a neighborhood called "Banesat e kuqe."[1] We were planning to go there while I noticed Adnan looking at us worried. The fact that the improvised mosque was in the basement of a building suggested that we had to carry Adnan down there and he felt guilty with the possibility of becoming a heavier burden to us.

'What are you thinking, Adnan?' Gazi asked him.

Adnan shrugged his shoulders. Gazi stared at him for a few seconds, then stood up and went toward him. He took Adnan's head in his hands, kissed him in his forehead and told him, with tears in his eyes:

'As long as I am around, you will be there with me.'

In this point Adnan felt comforted. However, deep inside him he knew he was a burden to us, especially to Gazi, although Gazi with his golden heart never gave a sign of tiredness.

---

[1] The red apartment buildings.

Chapter 6

The stairway to the basement was too narrow. We were trying hard to get it downstairs, but in vain. Adnan was begging to us:

'Send me back in the car! I can wait there until you finish.'

But Gazi didn't pay attention to his words, but went on trying. At a certain moment, I told Gazi to stop and listen to Adnan. It would be better even for Adnan to wait us in the car. But Gazi was very decisive. Then, Gazi showed Adnan his back and took him inside lifting him. All the people inside the improvised mosque were impressed by Gazi's behavior toward Adnan. The mosque was almost 99 percent filled with young boys and men. A young man with a middle beard offered to spray our hands with eau de cologne. All those present there were sprayed their hands with it, but the scent spread in the air was very strong and I would rather not take it.

The improvised mosque was full. After the Adh'an, the Imam came in the front. He didn't need any microphone because it was a small place we could hear him without any problem. The Imam climbed the improvised Minbar stairs. He was a bit fat for his height and found its way a bit difficult to the top of the stairs. He had a long beard and staring eyes giving the impression that he was a rough person. He had a strong voice too. He started to say his prayers and praise Allah with a harsh voice in Arabic. He hit the handrail with his punch to attract our attention. Then he wiped with his fingers the right corner of his lips, speaking at the same time trying to have our maximum attention. After wiping again the right corner of his lip he punched again the handrail and went on with a threatening voice. We were stunned. A strange silence ruled in the room. He went on:

'There is no doubt. The Truth is being heard all over the Globe and all Muslims are uniting their powers and their convictions. Soon, there will be only one language, one rule of law.'

Raising his right hand, showing his index finger he followed:

'The system of idolatry will die. The lifestyle that the West imposes you, you twerps, has died. What is the model of this lifestyle? What do you consider emancipation? What do you consider civilization? The immortal society created by the West, where everything is profiting, where conscience, mercy, honesty have no worth; where the values are only financial, where the rich tyrannize the working class; where work replaces family, where the individuals are isolated in order to be exploited like a lemon and thrown away; where the women are without control and the men marry in between them; where the human body is sold in front of all people without facing any reaction; where whole generations make a rudimentary living of cheating and impoverishing. Is this the pattern that this system is proud of? No, a house can't be built on the sea foams. The system of idolatry is rotting. It is stinking and it is infesting the air we breathe. We are able to see only its phantom being exposed with the light speed. We can't allow anymore that the Muslim blood pours like sewage. We can't allow anymore that the Muslims are slaughtered like animals. Enough with humiliating the Muslims! Enough is enough! I am addressing to the Imams to tell the Truth and not withdraw from it. They must say it openly the Muslim world is in open war with non Muslim world. The must say it openly that the oppressive non Muslims must be fought.'

I said to myself: 'What he is talking about? The men in the room were all sad. Adnan looked at the Imam stunned and his face was sad. Gazi had strengthen his jaws and one time he stared at the Imam and the other time looked on the ground, with his punches tightened nervously.

After the prayer, we waited for the rest to go out and then Gazi took Adnan on his back and headed toward the exit under the astonished eyes of the men and the young men who went out beforehand and we waiting outside.

'God Bless you!' Told someone Gazi behind his back and then he asked him and Adnan about their impressions regarding the Imam and the Friday prayers in that improvised mosque.

'It was ok, not so bad,' said Adnan, but his face expression was telling something else.

Gazi turned toward the young man and introduced himself.

'I am Fatlum,' replied the young man.

'It was nice to meet you. Regarding the question you asked Adnan, I would answer that the Imam was a real lion. I have never heard such a preaching during all this time we are frequenting the Friday prayer in different mosques. We need such men."

To tell the truth, I didn't like what Gazi was saying. On the contrary, Fatlum hugged him, saying to him:

'Well done, brave boy. The Imam needs young men like you.'

Agim didn't say a word. I remained silent too. Fatlum turned toward us, saying:

'I swear to God, we need brave men. The Muslims are suffering a merciless oppression.'

But only Gazi liked his word. Fatlum asked Gazi for his mobile number and invited him for coffee. In the car, Adnan asked for his favorite music and Gazi didn't reject. We weren't so happy with what had happened except Gazi. I didn't agree with the Imam's preaching. It was too harsh and instigating. If followed in practice, it would have caused a big affliction. I couldn't agree at all with what I heard that day in that mosque.

Chapter 7

It was half past ten in the morning. I was half awaked in an effort to go back to sleep. Suddenly the door opened. My mother came near my bad and kissed me in my forehead:

'Get up, Beni! Agim is waiting for you outside.'

Agim and I used to frequent each-other in turns almost every day, since the first grade until the last year of the middle school. As I didn't have any brothers, I would share every bit of my life with Agim, Gazi and Adnan and they considered me as their brother. We shared together our happy and our sad moments.

'Hurry up, you lazy boy! Our friends are waiting for us.'

'I will be ready in just a bit, Gimi.'

When we went to middle school we began to sit in coffee bars when we had money. It was not important who had the money. We used to go to our favorite coffee bar and discuss about different topics. Gazi was smart but he didn't read much. He was very sensitive but really helpful in need. He cried when I came back from Brussels worried that something bad might have happened to me. He would say:

'O God, destroy those filthy terrorists! Send them to hell! He cursed them and his eyes in tears repeating:

'How is it possible to kill innocent people?'

And then hugging me and saying:

'I love you so much, my brother!' Thanking continuously God I was alive.

I ordered the waiter:

'I want a strong coffee, please!'

Agim advised not to drink strong coffees. I called him "my personal doctor," joking with him. Gazi started saying:

'I was impressed by the Imam and his preaching in the improvised mosque. He was a brave man.'

'He was good, but a bit harsh,' replied Agim.

'It seemed to me harsh. His words were instigating, or not?' I asked.

'I think the same,' Adnan added.

Gazi didn't agree with us but we couldn't tell if he agreed with the Imam's words completely or not. Maybe he was not so clear because we were three against his opinion.

'I could understand that we are in war with anyone non Muslim,' continued Adnan.

I nodded. Agim cleared his voice and added:

'He made it clear: In war with all!'

Gazi was troubled, but he had himself under control. I knew his opinion from that Friday day, but I thought maybe our discussion would change his mind. Gazi was a discreet boy and couldn't understand him easily. The way of his thinking was a mystery. I was worried about him because I knew he was stubborn and I knew his past too. He was brought in a family with social problems. Anyway, anyone can have his own opinions unless he doesn't do any harm to the others.

Adnan was happy. His cousin from Germany, more precisely his uncle's son, had bought him a wheelchair with battery and it was due to be delivered to his home within the week. We were happy, but Gazi was the happiest of all. He kissed Adnan in his head and joked with him telling him that he would ride it to. Adnan looked him in his eyes and his smile hid his pain. We changed topic again when Gazi's mobile rang:

'Yes, ok. We can meet whenever you want, my brother.'

I could guess it was Fatlum, but I didn't ask Gazi about that.

We went on talking about Adnan's new wheelchair. We were curious about the details of the wheelchair. I was curious to know especially if the battery ended, whether we could push the wheelchair manually. Adnan didn't have any detailed information so he couldn't tell us anything. However, we all were happy that he finally could be somehow independent. It was more or less the same wheelchair a handicapped woman moved often around the city and Adnan looked at her envying her in secret. He never told us anything, because he knew it was too expensive and it was almost impossible for us to buy it.

Chapter 8

'Ok, but call Gazi and Adnan too. Ok, Beni?' Agim told me.

A sunny day we went to watch the football match, but Gazi didn't come. Adnan was enjoying his ride with his new wheelchair with battery:

'Come and catch!'

He was very happy and relieved with the idea that we were relieved from the burden to push his wheelchair.

'Will you let me ride it once?' I joked with him.

'Yes, but on a condition, Beni.'

'Ok.'

'If you catch me...'

The race began. I could catch him, but I didn't want to spoil his fun. Instead, I told him I was tired. He laughed so happily as if though he could walk. I thanked God for making me able to walk, in the meantime I felt sorry for him. He was waiting for us some meters ahead. I began to think: What if he someday he will be able to walk? How much happy will he be? Why don't I thank God enough about this great grace He gave me? If Adnan is so happy about being finally somehow independent because of riding a wheelchair with battery, what about me that I can move freely and I can go wherever I want, I can play football, table tennis and perform endless activities independently?

Agim went to buy the tickets while we were going toward the crowd waiting outside, in front of the stadium entrance. I was walking behind Adnan. People let us go through because of him. Even when we went inside, there were some boys offered to swap with us their seats on the first row. We thanked them. Some people show their humanity when they see handicapped people. Thank God there are still people like that. Our football team fans shouted "shoot, shoot!" Adnan was shouting passionately like he had played football. I was stunned how was it possible he was so excited in the meantime his foot never touched a ball. I felt really sorry for him.

After the match, we went to the usual coffee bar. Fatlum was there too. He was very a bit arrogant especially when we began to talk about religious topics:

'Waiter turn off that music! You are driving us crazy with it. Don't you know it is haram?'

He told the waiter, but the waiter replied:

'The sound is normal. Besides, we can't turn it off, because these are the coffee bar rules.'

'Shame on you! Your behavior is inacceptable. Your are corrupting the youth with loud music and alcoholic drinks.

The waiter remained surprised looking at Fatlum, who was raising his voice, blushing and raising his index finger:

'Sorry, but I am just an employee,' he replied to him.

'Isn't it haram to earn your living selling alcohol? Fatlum added.

All people in the coffee bar were staring at us. Agim, Adnan and I remained stunned and Gazi remained speechless with his eyes on the floor. In the meantime, the owner came.

'Calm down, young man! Everyone has his own way of doing things. If my coffee bar seems inappropriate to your tastes you are free to go where it suits you better. But please, as long as you sit here, don't disturb my clients!' He told Fatlum.

'It's my fault I entered this filthy place. Stand up, Gazi! Let's get out of here!' Fatlum stood up and was about to go out.

We knew the owner very well. He remained calm until Fatlum and Gazi went out, without saying "goodbye." After a while, we were about to leave too. When we tried to apologize, the owner told us not to worry because it wasn't our fault. On our way home we showed our surprise about Fatlum loosing his temper like that. After all, we are human beings.

Chapter 9

I was alone at home. My mother and Besa had gone to visit my aunt in the countryside. I was reading a book. Afërdita preferred to visit me instead of going shopping with her mother. It had been two days since I hadn't seen her. I heard the door opening and saw Afërdita came in. We were together for one year and a half. Maybe we were too young to marry but I loved her so much. She had become the half of me. She was an intelligent and a humble girl. She was very beautiful with light brown hair and big, blue eyes. We sat on the sofa where I was reading the book. She saw the book, took it and asked me:

'Did you finish it?'

'Three pages left.' I answered.

'Finish them. I can wait.' She added.

'I can't concentrate on the book while I feel your scent.' I replied, taking away the book from her hand and leaving it on the table. I took her by her hands and pulled her toward me. She wanted to say something but I didn't let her. I put my hand on her shoulder and she hid her head on my left shoulder. We asked each-other about our respective families. Then I told her about Adnan and his new wheelchair. I saw tears in her eyes. I took her by her head and kissed her on her forefront.

She closed her eyes, but her tears dropped over her cheeks. I wiped her tears with my thumbs. I stared at her wonderful face and I couldn't help but kissing her on her beautiful eyes and squeezed her against my body. I said I loved her and she said she loved me too. We talked about marriage and having children. Suddenly I stared at the wall in front of me while she kept staring at me:

'Beni, aren't we too young to marry and have children?' I laughed silently relieving my breath out.

I stared at her eyes for almost ten seconds.

'Why are you looking at me like that, Beni?' She asked me.

'I can't wait until we marry.' I answered.

'Beni, I need to finish our studies. Maybe we are too young to marry now.' She replied.

'You are right, my sweetheart, but I love you so much, so maybe we can hurry a bit. Anyway, you are right. It's better to finish our studies first then think of marriage.' I agreed with her.

'Beni, how do you feel now?' Afërdita asked me.

'Besa and I are fine, but Fjona is recovered to psychiatric hospital. We are worried about her. Curse on those crazy people! They destroy other people's life. Definitely, they are senseless people. Sweetheart, can we change topic because I don't feel well when I recall that day.' I had begun to tremble.

'Of course, Beni.' She didn't want me to worry then she changed the topic of conversation. 'Who won the match?'

Chapter 10

'I invited you. Dare not to come!' Gazi said to me.

'Are you threatening me?' I laughed loudly.

'Take it as you like it, but you must come.' Gazi replied to me.

'Ok, but who will be there?' I asked him again.

'You, Adnan, Agim, Fatlum and Kujtim.' He answered me.

Gazi lived with his mother, aunt Bukurie, and his brother, Kujtim. His mother had been divorced from his father since Gazi was six years old due to heavy problems with alcohol. Gazi's family had suffered a real trauma because of that.

Gazi's mother opened us the door.

'Welcome, my boys! How are you?' And then she turned toward me. 'Beni, how is Gona? I missed her. I will come someday to your house to visit her. You have a wonderful mother. She is a real lady.'

'Thank you, aunt Bukurie.' I replied to her.

'How are you, Adnan? How is your family?' She went on with Adnan.

'We are ok, thank you.' Adnan replied.

After she greeted Agim and Fatlum too, she went on chatting with us while Gazi and Kujtim were making ready the dinner table. She thanked us for being good friends to Gazi, whose health was delicate because a serious illness he had had in his early childhood and staying in hospitals in long terms. She was very worried about him. She wanted eagerly to see him graduated and then married with children:

'Will my dreams be fulfilled one day?' Her heart as a mother couldn't find peace.

'Don't worry,' I atold her. 'All your dreams will be fulfilled one day.'

'God bless you, Beni!' And then she went on. 'Sorry, boys, but I need to and help Gazi and Kujtim in the kitchen. You will have dinner together, because I need to visit a friend of mine. Feel relaxed! This is your home too.'

We thanked her. In the meantime, Adnan wanted to go to the toilet and Gazi helped him. Kujtim told us Gazi's worries about Adnan. Once when they were watching a documentary about terrorism, they saw mutilated people and Gazi was very angry with the people who dared do such things to other people and cursed them.

'When there are no other means to take revenge for the injustices suffered, such acts are somehow allowed.' Fatlum interfered, but me and Agim told him that it was unacceptable to pressure a government by killing and mutilating innocent people.

Gazi came back together with Adnan:

'There are trials everywhere.' He complained.

Fatlum replied:

'Trials are useful and we must be patient, because we are rewarded according to our patience.' Replied Fatlum and he went on. 'According to Imam Beka, the Prophets were most afflicted people were, then the Good people, and so on. We must endure any trial in our life, so to reach the Prophets and Good People in degree. One day I had a heated debate with my parents. They tell me not to tell the Truth. They are unbelievers and they don't pray but they want to teach me about the

Truth. Imam Beka has taught us to protect the Truth. The interesting fact is that people try to turn me away from what Imam Beka taught me but I tend more and more to support his teachings. The Prophets were afflicted because they protected the Truth too.'

Fatlum was very convinced in his words. He spoke like he knew all the religious explanations. But I tried to make him use his logic:

'I think you haven't understood properly the right meaning of "trial" and "patience" in religion.' I tried to make him listen to reason. 'Not always we have to insist or even to be patient with the excuse that we are afflicted by a trial. We are human beings and we don't have to take all the troubles in life as afflictions. The Prophets of God knew well how to understand a real trial because they were Godsend. We can't compare ourselves to them. We are normal human beings who make mistakes.'

Fatlum got very agitated and made uncontrolled movements. Blushing and embarrassed he said:

'Fear God and repent to Him! You are contradicting Imam Beka's words, a religious savant of our region.' Aftwr a while, he added. 'I have to go.'

And he left without saying anything else. Gazi was very sad but didn't say anything. It was obvious, Fatlum left because of my words. Meanwhile, Kujtim said:

'If he went away because he didn't like Beni's words, no problem. Well done for your courage Beni!'

Adnan and Agim nodded while Gazi looked on the floor, a gesture he would every time he didn't agree with something. Fatlum had become a best friend to Gazi and Gazi didn't like the fact that someone might hurt Fatlum's feelings.

Chapter 11

One Sunday morning my mother invited Besa, Afërdita and me to have dinner at a restaurant by the lake shore. The view by the lake was breathtaking. Seagulls were flying over the lake waters. Some fish boats cradled by the lake waves near the shore in wait to go for fishing the next morning.

My mother felt nostalgic when she came to that same restaurant because she used to dine with my father there when he was alive. Also the restaurant was famous in my city for the fish delicacies. My mother cooked fish at home once a week. Bass was her favorite fish. My mother liked to read too and she was a religious woman.

'When you teach me about Islam, you tell me that I am not a believer until I am pious to my family, friends and society.' I said to her.

'Yes, Beni, I have said that.' She said.

'You have said also that a person is a good believer when the others feel relaxed in his presence.'

'Yes, these are the words of Prophet Mohammad. I just passed his word.'

'Dear mother, you have to me that 'Islam' means 'peace' and every thought, judgment or action that comes from Islam must be peace, love, harmony, tolerance, because the religion's purpose it to live in peace and harmony with others despite the religious, national and racial differences.' I went on.

'Yes and otherwise is against Islam and maybe is done with an evil purpose.' My mother replied to me.

'Mother, you also told me that a good Muslim must be well educated, isn't it?'

'Yes but you can be a good Muslim even if you aren't highly educated. The key is your heart. But a well educated Muslim is a fulfilled Muslim, because God in Holy Book says: There are not the same those who know from those who don't know…' Then she asked me. 'Why did you open this discussion now?'

Besa and Afërdita were listening attentively. My mother was a very good teacher so she knew very well the art of communication with people, especially with her own children.

'I don't want to hide anything from you. The point is that you speak positively about religion but when I hear other people speak about it I face dilemmas. What happened in Brussels and Imam Beka's preaching make me thing that want to make us believe that we are allowed to kill and discredit all people that think differently from us and all that contradicts your humble teachings about Islam.' I said to her.

'Yes my son, as you know your grandfather was an Imam and I took a lot from him.' She added.

'Yes I know.' I replied to her.

'And I read a lot. Also I always ask my friend Aishe when it comes to religious issues.'

Aisha is my mother's friend and she has a master degree for Islamic Sciences and lectures in a prestigious university in Lion. My mother went on:

'Once during her lecture Aisha was asked by a student whether it was needed or not reformation in Islam. Aisha was categorically against any reformation regarding the Holy Koran and the Islam, but it is the Muslim community that needs reformation and the interpretation of Koran and Islam.'

'But mother, how is it possible that in Islam there are imams that promote violence in the name of Islam? Imam Beka was behaving arrogantly in an effort to push us against West. You have told me that there is no place in Jannah for a Muslim who shows even a particle of arrogance.' I insisted.

'The problem is that they are detached from the reality and the world we live in. They read a certain literature that they find it suitable for themselves and accept another truth other than that. They might be highly educated but they are narrow-minded. They have a subjectivist prospective of the reality instead of an objectivist one' She tried to explain to me.

'O God, protect us from the ignorant with master degrees!' I prayed.

'My son, you are nineteen years old and Besa twelve years old. I sacrificed everything to raise you. Take care of yourselves! Don't fall pray of manipulative people that claim God reward for killing innocent people! In fact, it will happen the opposite thing. They will be punished harshly for their doings in the Day of the Judgment. Allah said in the Koran: Who kills an innocent person it is as if killed the entire humanity and who saves an innocent person it is as if he saved the entire humanity...' My mother cited the Holy Koran to support her idea.

'Don't worry mother! I will not follow prey of those groups. Instead I will save others who fall prey to their clutches.' I tried to comfort my mother.

'I have faith in you, my son.' My mother said.

The fish had become cold but it was still delicious. Afërdita enjoyed the dinner and the discussion between me and my mother. She was very discreet out of respect for my mother and never spoke too much in front of her.

'Thank you for the dinner and your valuable word, aunt Gone!' She said.

Suddenly the mobile rang:

'Beni, did you hear the news?' I could understand by the voice that it was Agim.

'No, what happened?' I asked him.

'Fatlum was arrested. He bit a person while going out of Sahat Kulla mosque. They sent him in the hospital in serious conditions.' He said.

'What about Gazi?' I asked him.

'Gazi is ok but I am calling him again and then I will call you again.' And he hung up.

'What happened?' My mother asked, extremely worried.

'Gazi's friend, Fatlum, was arrested. Nothing serious.' I tried to re-assure her.

'Do you know him?' She asked me.

'I have met him only twice but I could understand he had extremist ideas.' I explained to my mother.

Agim rang again:

'I just talked to Gazi on the phone. He had an argument with the victim because of a Bid'ah. He lost his temper and attacked him mer-cilessly.'

'How is the victim's health?' I asked Agim.

'He had his jaw displaced and had a wound in his head.' He ex-plained me.

'I am sorry about that poor boy. We need to meet Gazi tomorrow at 10:00.' I said to him.

'Ok I will tell him right now. See you!' Agim said.

'See you!' And I hung up.

My mother petted me on my head. I understood and said to her:

'Don't worry, my dear mother! I will never do anything that worries you.'

Chapter 12

'Coffee, please!' We ordered.

'What happened to Fatlum?' I asked Gazi.

Gazi didn't answer but kept looking on the floor as usual when he wanted to escape the situation.

'Fatlum is a rough boy.' Agim said.

But Adnan couldn't say anything although it was obvious he shared the same opinion with us as always because he didn't want to go against Gazi who was there for him all the time.

'I understood he wasn't suitable to be our friend that evening at your house.' I explained.

'Enough! Fatlum is a brave boy and fights for the Truth. He isn't nor rough neither dangerous. I am worried he is arrested, you speak me like that about him.' Gazi was angry with us.

We changed topic but I was surprised. Gazi was protecting Fatlum that he knew from a short period of time and didn't apologize to us for his behavior. Gazi invited us to the Akik ceremony of Albion, a friend of him at the mosque of the basement. He had a baby boy so he was going to sacrifice two muttons. To tell the truth I didn't like the idea he frequented that mosque but I didn't tell him anything. I accepted to go because I wanted to understand the extremist mentality of the group Gazi was attracted to and supported so eagerly. Agim found an excuse not to go.

Gazi said that he had to go somewhere and he left. We stayed and talked. We needed to keep and protect each-other. The world outside was harsh.

Suddenly my phone rang:

'Yeah, Gazi?'

'Beni, the Akik will be held at our friend's house.'

'Ok see you then!' I said to him.

Chapter 13

Gazi came to take me with his car. During the ride he spoke me very highly about Imam Beka. When we arrived at Gazi's friend house we took off our shoes and greeted with Salam Alaykum and our host replied Wa Alaykum Salam. Gazi introduced us to him. He called him Abu Yusuf. His name suggested he was from an Arab country who spoke Albanian. Gazi told me that his name had been Arian, a non Muslim name and if you are a Muslim you shouldn't be named by a non Muslim name.

'What about our names?' I asked him.

'They have good meaning so they are allowed.' He answered.

'Then why he didn't change his name into an Albanian name?' I insisted.

But Gazi lost his temper as always and instead told to go inside. We sat on the ground impressed that nobody stood up to say "hello!" My mother had taught us that it impolite not to stand up when guests come into a room where you are staying. I asked Gazi in a low voice:

'Why they didn't stand up?'

He didn't say a word but seemed angry. I understood he got annoyed because of my questions and I remained silent. Imam Beka began his speech by advising the guests to pay attention with who they make friends. In that moment someone raised his hand to ask a question, carefully and a bit scared. Imam Beka got annoyed and spoke to him with an irritated voice:

'Speak!'

The boy said that he was reading a book about religion by a certain author, an Imam and Alim. Beka lost his temper:

'What are you talking about? Who are you calling Imam and Alim? As soon as you arrive home, throw the book in fire! And don't read anymore authors like that, ok?'

'Ok.' Said the boy blushed in his face.

Then Imam Beka went on with his preaching:

'Did you know that your parents or your family members that don't pray are considered Kafirs?'

'O my God.' I said to myself, 'How is it possible that my sister is a Kafir?'

My logic didn't accept his words. He went on:

'Did you know that mustn't make friendship with believers of other religions?'

I was terrified. We had some good Christian neighbors. My mother used to drink the morning coffee with aunt Mrika and Besa was best friend with her daughter, Maria. We celebrated each-other religious feasts and we respected each-other. From the preaching of Imam Beka and other Imams like him I could make the difference between the Right Path and radical ideology that caused tragedies like the terrorist act I almost fell victim together with my beloved ones.

'Take it!' A boy with a long beard and Taqiyah (cap) gave me a plastic plate with rice and meat from mutton sacrificed.

I began to eat and thinking about the rude behavior of Imam Beka and his harsh way of preaching which was against what I had heard from other Imams and from my mother. His main purpose was to prevent his group from reading different books so he could control them. His logic was isolating his followers. He wanted to impose to his group reading only the books he wanted them to read, detaching them from the world, from information in general, in order to brainwash and indoctrinate them. I was chewing my thoughts together with the meat I was taking from the plastic plate in front of me when I heard him raising his voice:

'Fear Allah! Allah can punish you severely in Hell. Allah can destroy you in a blink of an eye.'

I got scared. Everyone there remained stunned from his frightful screaming. I looked at Gazi. He looked stunned and frightened. His face was pale. His hands were trembling. I said to myself: O my God, You are the Merciful. Your mercy prevails over Your wrath. You are not violent and harsh as this idiot - claiming to be an Imam - is introducing you. You have poured over Earth one of Your hundred mercies. You are not like this ignorant id depicting you. He knows nothing but screaming. O God forgive us, because you are the Forgiver!

I went on saying prayers until I began to tremble too. How was it possible that my mother, who didn't study theology, spoke about God as a good, merciful and graceful God, only angry and punishing God with evil and oppressive people. I felt like Imam Beka was one of those who wanted to bring affliction into the Earth. He was the one who didn't deserve respect and not those people from other religions. In the meantime, Imam Beka asked the audience arrogantly:

'Do you have any question?'

One of his followers, who was dozing most of the time, began to praise him and his speech:

'Well done, Imam! Your speech was brilliant.'

I was sure he didn't hear thirty per cent of the speech. Imam Beka closed his speech. We prayed in the end and left. I and Gazi headed home. Suddenly Gazi said to me:

'I told you, you get goose-bumps when you hear his speeches.'

'Do you really believe that his knowledge about religion is right?' I asked him.

'Of course yes.' He said.

'In three ours we stayed there he never mentioned "mercy", "peace", "love", only but "violence", "punishment", "hell." Gazi, my dear friend, beware of that man! I don't know much about religion however I can understand that this man has nothing to do with the real Islam.' I tried to explain.

'What are you saying? ' Gazi got very angry.

'We are best friends and I must tell you the truth no matter what.' I said to him.

'How dare you speak like that about a prestigious Imam like Imam Beka?' It was clear he had lost his reasoning.

In the meantime, we reached Gazi's home. I said to him:

'Salam Alaykum!'

'Wa Alaykum Salam!' He replied almost whispering.

He had become more and more aggressive. He didn't care that we were best friends since the childhood. I wanted to solve this issue once forever so I called Agim before I arrived home. He was surprised by my urgency and asked me for explanations but I wanted to talk with him face to face. Besa opened the door to. My mother was reading. I went to her and hugged her. She looked at me worried and asked:

'Has anything happened to you?'

'No, I am just a bit tired.' I said her.

In the meantime, I heard Agim's voice at the door.

We entered my room. I told him about what happened at Akik and

I told him about Imam Beka. But the most, I was worried about Gazi. Agim was worried too. We decided to invite him for coffee tomorrow and talk to him. We would meet tomorrow at 11:00. After seeing off Agim I went to sleep exhausted. I had a bad headache so I took a pill although it had been sometime I hadn't taken them.

Chapter 14

I reached at our favorite bar beforehand. After a while Agim came. We sat at the table in the corner where we used to sit. We needed a new approach with Gazi. He had changed a lot, on an exception. He was more emotional. This was dangerous for him because now on he was overruled by his emotions not by his reason. Ne needed to talk him softly if we wanted him to listen to our words. I told Agim to call him because I thought Gazi was angry with me and maybe he wouldn't accept to come. He finally came though not willingly. He greeted us:

'Asalamu Alaykum! How are you my brothers? What's up?'

I was very glad that he wasn't angry with me at all. He looked fine.

'We are ok? What about you? Do you have any news from Fatlum?'

'I went to the police station and a policeman rebuked us for overdoing regarding the religion. I told him that If I were in Fatlum's place I would beat that person too. We don't want Bid'ahs in Islam. The policeman was about to arrest me to. I wish I could cut his head! I have seen him when he comes at the Friday prayers. The hypocrite! When I see him next time in the mosque I will tell him in front of all 'qafir, you will rot in hell, it's my duty to kill you' to discredit him.' He said to us.

'Gazi, what are you talking about the policeman that risks his life for our safety? Let alone, as you are saying, he is a believer in Islam. How dare you say 'qafir' to a believer? Even if he doesn't pray regularly he is willing to sacrifice his life for our sake.' I said to him.

'He obeys the State's Law and not Allah's Law.' He replied to me.

'Why? You don't obey them anymore?' I asked him.

'Jo, it's haram to respect other laws than God's Laws.' He answered me.

'Does Fatlum have a lawyer?' I asked him changing topic.

'Yes, and he said that Fatlum may be sentenced six month to one year in jail. The justice of the devil' He said me.

'That's why we must be careful with our behavior.' I tried to advice him.

'You name this whatever you want but I will never cease protecting the Word of God.' He almost lost his temper.

In order not to escalate the situation and not ruin the friendship with him, we decided to leave. I tried to shake hands with him but he withdrew his hand telling me:

'I tolerate you because we have grown up together. You are a good boy and I have faith in you. Come to our meetings with Imam Beka more often so you can understand the real Truth.' He said to me.

'I love you too as my best friend. I promise, I will come to Imam Beka's preaching.' I said to him.

We hugged each-other and Gazi left. Agim and I had a walk by the riverside. We decided to take Adnan too because it was a beautiful weather. Adnan was enjoying his new wheelchair. He didn't feel anymore that much embarrassed for being a burden to us.

Chapter 15

After four days I had to keep my promise and to Imam Beka's preaching. Agimi didn't want to come. He was categorical if he didn't like something, but I was still curious and I wanted to help Gazi change his mind. I didn't know the location where the preaching was about to be held and I called Gazi.

'Do you remember the football field in the Martyrs Neighborhood?' He asked me.

'Yes I remember.' I said to him.

'Walk twenty meters past the stadium and turn right! On your left you will walk another thirty meters until a Grocery Store. There you may ask about Sadiq and they will tell you where he lives. We are waiting for you.' He explained me.

'Ok Gazi.' And I hung on.

I finally arrived at the Grocery Store. When I asked the man there he looked at me a bit surprised:

'He lives in that house there with the brown door. How do you know him?'

'He is my friend.' I answered him to avoid any further comment.

'Ok.' He said to me looking into my eyes.

I began asking myself why he behaved like that. I knocked at the door but the shopkeeper told me to ring the bell which was somewhere on the side of the door. Sadik opened the door.

'Hello! I am Beni, Gazi's friend.' I introduced myself.

'Yes, come in!' He said to me.

I had imagined him tall but he was a small man with a wide forefront, half bald. He had a beard not as long as Imam Beka's. We entered his house and Gazi made me a sign to sit nearby him. I didn't want because if I sat nearby him he wouldn't let me ask Imam Beka, but I sat where he wanted anyway.

Imam hadn't come yet, so Gazi took the opportunity to introduce me to the people in the room. This time there were thirty people. And I was surpised by the fact that only two of them had graduated from university. Gazi told me that four of them had been living abroad and were former criminals but now they are on the right path, thank God! I had heard about some boys with disturbed past but I had never met them. Gazi told me that six of those in the room lived in extreme poverty. Then we began to talk freely. Someone mentioned the Virgins of Paradise. He didn't want two or three but all the seventy two promised if you fal martyr, so he preferred to fall martyr. In that moment Agron began to speak. He was the deputy of Imam Beka. He had changed his name into Anas Talab. With a gloomy face and arrogant movement he raised his hand to silent the audience. From a relaxed and joyous atmosphere it became like a funeral atmosphere. He addressed to the boy:

'First of all you shouldn't joke with religious matters. Secondly to deserve the seventy two Virgins you must be a man.'

'I am a man.' The boy said to him.

'I am the deputy of Imam Beka and you mustn't interrupt me when I am speaking.' He replied to him and his voice became harsher.

'I am sorry. I just joked because I thought we are brothers and we can be relaxed in the presence of each-other.' The boy said.

'You can't joke with religious matters. A man is not someone with a genital of a man but someone who dies for Allah's sake. Did you understand now how you can win the seventy two Virgins?' Anas Talab went on.

I raised my hand.

'Do you have any question?' He addressed me.

'My question is: We can't be granted seventy two Virgins other than by fighting and dying in a religious fighting can we?' I asked him.

'This is a question made by cowards with a male genital but sensitive like females.' He said to me.

The audience laughed, but not like the first time. This time it was Anas Talab "joking".' I blushed. I felt like the ceiling was falling over my head. I was covered in sweat embarrassed. However I insisted:

'As I know a person can fall martyr even lying in his bed, isn't it so?'

'Yes it is.' He softened his speech.'

'You are considered a martyr if you die in an accident, if you are drowned, if you fall victim of an earthquake, if you die from stomach complications and so on and so forth, not only when you fight in a war. Why don't you explain us these? Why don't you explain us the maters as they are factually?' I insisted.

I felt pain on my toes. Gazi was pressing me with his hand. Anas Talab wasn't feeling comfortable with my comments and my questions. His face changed color. He got nervous. He cleared his voice and asked me:

'How old are you?'

'I am eighteen years old and a half.' I answered.

'Of course you aren't married, are you?' He went on with his question.

'No I am not.' I went on with my answers.

'Men like you are as cowards as to keep their wives bareheaded.' He said to me.

'What should I do in such a situation according to you?' I asked him.

'Order her to cover her head or divorce her!' He raised his voice.

'Divorce her, even if we have children together?' I remained shocked.

'When it comes to Allah's Law family comes next. You are speaking too much. That's why I need to raise my voice with you.' He said to me.

'This would be an imposition. The imposition is forbidden in Islam. The imposed actions would lack sincerity and that would be unacceptable by God.' I tried to explain my point.

He wanted to say something but Imam Beka came in and greeted us with 'Salam Alaykum" and went on the front next to Anas Talab. We replied him with "We Alaykum Salam." He asked the audience with arrogance and pride:

'How are you?'

'Ok, Al-Hamdul-lAh.' They answered smiling and somehow scared of him.

'Today I will speak about Jihad.' He said and looked at me like I was a sinner.

I felt uncomfortable. He stared at me for a few minutes then went on:

'Will you ask questions like you did in the last occasion?'

'If you let me, because I want to know more about Islam.' I said to him.

'Ok but you asked more than you should.' He replied to me.

'Maybe but…' He interrupted me by waving his hand.

Then he began his speech:

'My Muslim brothers, you very well the affliction caused to Muslims by the enemies of Islam. There are killings and bloodshed everywhere where Muslims live. The enemies of Islam aren't sparing the harshest methods of mistreatment against Muslims. Dear brothers, other Muslims shouldn't be in peace with themselves while elsewhere their brothers and sisters, including children, are being killed by the enemies of Islam.'

I heard a sobbing nearby me. Gazi was crying. I wanted to talk to him but he waved his hand forbidding me to do so. I looked around. Only almost the third of us wasn't crying although we were shocked too.

'… So it is necessary to act. We know there is a possibility how to revenge against those oppressors. So who considers himself a real man he must know that the reward of Allah for the Jihad is huge. You must talk about this with your friends and family members. Today the holly Jihad is obligatory for every Muslim.' He finally went to his point.

He was speaking without illustrating his speech with facts and official data. He even justified his words by using verses from the Quran and sayings from the Prophet. He could say whatever he wanted because his audience wasn't made neither by intellectuals nor by educated people. I received the answer for my question. I just saw with my own eyes and I just heard with my own ears how ordinary people were being manipulated and sent astray in the name of Islam. First of all, they had selected uneducated young men and men possibly economically poor and with social problems. And they tried to radicalize them through the so called Imams like Imam Beka by brainwashing them and guiding them like robots with the purpose to use them as kamikazis when needed. I took the opportunity to ask him again:

'Is it so simple to qualify the Jihad? Because as far as I know this is not the exact definition of Jihad.' I insisted.

He wasn't used to be objected. He said in a rudely and ironically:

'Tell us the definition of Jihad according to you?'

'I don't know it exactly but I will ask someone who knows it and I will tell you next time.' I said to him.

'Yes but ask a real man!' He replied.

'What qualifies a real man?' I asked him surprised.

'His beard.' He answered firmed.

'Not necessarily.' I insisted.

'Yes, in most cases.' He raised his voice.

I wanted to reply but he went on:

I finished my higher studies for Islamic Jurisprudence and I know what I am saying. I don't need the opinions of the cowards that call themselves Imams. I am not afraid to speak the Truth like most people do today. Are we watching every day how the Muslim children are being killed and tortured? What if they were our children?

'Allah Aqbar!' I was shocked by the scream.

'Allah Aqbar!' The audience replied.

I deducted that those people were brainwashed and they would act emotionally in a given situation in the future. Any further question was worthless. I wasn't paying attention to Imam Beka's word anymore. When we left Sadiq's house, Gazi rebuked me:

'Try to ask worthy questions next time!'

I could understand now why Gazi lost his reason. I was sure everyone that followed Imam Beka's reunions would commit terrorist attacks if Imam Beka asked him to.

'What is a worthy question? Because I ask to know something not what suits the other person.' I said to him.

Gazi was very nervous and was walking fast to get rid of me as soon as possible.

'Gazi, I want to tell you something.' I said to him before leaving him. 'Go away from that group! Following Imam Beka you will cause harm to yourself, to your friends and family, and to society. You are my best friend and I want your best. You can't expect anything good from an arrogant person like him who thinks he knows everything. Don't go astray because you might suffer a bitter end. We both love Islam but don't let anyone to destroy you in the name of Islam. We should ask a real Imam for religious issues such as Jihad. For the last time I am asking you, don't follow that Imam!' I tried to persuade him.

Gazi with tears in his eyes Gazi said to me:

'I am in the right path and I am sorry for you. Imam Beka has said, according Mohammad the Prophet of God the Muslim Ummah will be divided in seventy three groups and only one of them with be in Jannah and the others will be in Jahannam. So come with me until it's not too late!'

'How come you think that the group that will enter the Jannah is the group of uneducated and ignorant people that are guided by their emotions and not their reason, that are isolated from the world and kill innocent people while this is categorically forbidden to Muslims. They look the reality with gloomy glasses and misbehave with their parents though God and His Prophet ordered us to respect them. Gazi, do you understand he brainwashed you?' I went on in an effort to make him come into his senses.

'You know what? I have chosen my path. You can follow yours' He said to me and looked me like he was going to die.

Then he turned his back to me and left without giving 'Salam.'

Chapter 16

The next day I met with Agim at our favorite coffee bar.

'So I was right not to come.' He said to me.

'You know with what purpose I went there.' I explained to him.

'We can't let Gazi in that man's hands. He needs our help now more than ever.' Agim was seriously worried about Gazi.

'That Imam Beka and the most of his group have strange ideas. He claims that Jihad is only war against enemies of Islam. He only was trying to insitigate the Muslim youth against the non-Muslims. He was speaking like the main mission of Islam was violence not peace. The audience cried when he spoke. He is able to manipulate his audience. And you know what? When I asked a shopkeeper where Sadiq's house was, he looked at me in a strange way.' I recalled in the end.

'Maybe they are suspicious people.' He said to me.

'Yes some of them had been in prison abroad and some others had criminal past even in our country. That might be dangerous too.' I went on when my phone rang;

'This is State Police speaking! Are we speaking to Arben Lushaj?' I heard a man voice speaking.

'Yes, it's me.' I answered.

'Can you come to the coffee bar "Alba" in an hour? We need to speak with you.' He explained.

I went there on time. The detective came a few minutes after me. He greeted me like we knew eath-other for ages and introduced himself:

'My name is Skender, and I am a detective.'

'Nice to meet you! My name is Beni.' I introduced myself, feeling uncomfortable.

'I know who you are, Beni. Just relax. I am a police officer and my job is to guarantee security for the citizens of this country, including you.' He showed me his distinctive to calm me down.

'May I ask you, why you invited me here? I have never had to do with the police.' I tried to clear my situation.

'Relax Beni. I know who you are. Your mother is the best elementary school-teacher in town. Your father passed away when you and your sister Besa were too young. You are an intelligent and a polite boy. Let me tell you that your mother was my elementary school teacher.' He said to me.

I felt relieved. He went on:

'You were yesterday evening at a meeting in Sadiq's house. He has a criminal record. Also other people in that room are former criminals. The problem is not that those people are practicing Islam. We are concerned about their radical extremist views. They may become very dangerous. Be careful! To tell the truth I was informed that you didn't support their ideology in their meetings. You seem very clear minded. Well done! Today I invited you to tell me your impressions and your opinion about that group.'

'They are extremists in their ideas. They are a closed group. They think collectively not individually, directed by their leader, Imam Beka.' I explained to him.

'Do you remember anything particular about anyone of them?' He asked me.

'I don't know them in particular except Gazi. He is my friend.' I said to him.

'Do you think he might become dangerous?' He asked me.

'Gazi might enter into e physical conflict, but nothing more. I know him since our childhood. He will repent and go away from that group.' I answered him.

'I hope so.' He said to me, a bit perplexed.

'Be sure about that! I know Gazi well.' I tried to reassure him though I wasn't so sure myself.

'Ok Beni here is my card with my phone number. You can call me! And don't tell anyone about our meeting, ok?' He said to me.

'Ok.' I replied to him.

'Goodbye, then!' And he stood up to leave.

'Goodbye, officer!' I said, in the meantime I felt relieved that everything went well somehow.

Chapter 17

The next morning the mobile ring woke me up. After a few seconds I heard Agim's voice:

'Are you still sleeping?' He asked me.

'How is it possible that I am answering you, then?' I answered half in jest.

'Wake up, you big sleeper!' He said to me.

'What time is it?' I asked him.

'It is 9:15 o'clock.' He said to me.

'I will be ready in half an hour.' And I hung up.

We went to another coffee bar and I began to tell him about my meeting with the detective. I was well aware that my conversation with him was confidential but I had to share it with Agim because we were both concerned with the situation created. Agim agreed with me too that the groupthink was a dangerous thing.

'He asked me about Gazi too.' I went on telling Agim about my conversation with the detective.

'What did you say about him?' Agim asked me worried about our friend.

'I told him that Gazi is a good boy and he will come into his senses sooner or later.' I tried to reassure Agim.

'I am surprised why he asked you about Gazi specifically.' He insisted.

'I don't know exactly, anyway we must take care of Gazi before it is too late.' I replied to him.

Then we changed topic:

'Have you met with Afërdita?' Agim asked me.

'No since the day we had dinner together with my family.' I said to him. 'What about you? Have you got a crush on someone?'

'I don't want to think about girls until I finish my studies.' He said to me.

He had some strict thoughts about marriage. He thought that he had to find a good job first and then to get married but I was in love and I thought that finding love had nothing to do with economic situation.

Chapter 18

I was awakened by the ringtone of my phone.

'Where are you Beni? It's been three days we don't see each-other.' I heard the beloved voice of Afërdita on the other side.

'Afërdita, my sweetheart, I am sorry!' I tried to apologize.

Of course in these three days we talked on the phone and exchanges text messages but it seemed that she missed me more than that. I had missed her too. We met at our favorite coffee bar near our middle school where we used to meet since we met. At ten o'clock I was there.

'I missed you Beni. You can't imagine how much I love you.' She looked a bit worried.

'It's better not to see each-other for a few days so you can express your love more often.' I tried to joke with her.

I love you Beni!' She said to me.

'I love you too Afërdita!' I tried to comfort her.

'Where have you been these days?' She went on.

'I have been really busy. What about you? How have you been? How are you doing with your studies?' I asked her.

'I haven't been studying so much. I feel a bit blocked lately. I kept thinking about you.' She said to me.

I pushed her toward me. She was my medicine. When she was nearby me I would forget about all my worries. She filled me with positive energy. I felt another person after every meeting with her. I loved her. I loved her beautiful blue eyes. I loved her nice mole over the right corner of her lip. And I loved her for her eloquence. I loved her for her intelligence. After my mother, she was my best adviser.

'Beni last night I had a dream like we separated our wedding day. I couldn't sleep. I even cried.' She told me.

'It was just a dream, my sweetheart. I am here and I will always be there for you. We are inseparable.' I tried to comfort her.

'Promise me you will never leave me!' She said to me.

'I even can't think of such thing. Don't worry! It was just a bad dream. That's all. I love you so much!' I replied to her.

We promised each-other that only death would set us apart. Suddenly, I heard my phone ringing.

'Hello Beni Where are you? It's been a long time.' I heard Taulant's voice on the other side.

'Hello Taulant! I am drinking coffee with my fiancée, my beautiful princess.' I said proudly.

'Beni I want to talk to you about a serious issue. When you finish give me a ring so we can meet together.' Taulant insisted.

I saw off Afërdita near her house and went to Taulant family's coffee bar to meet with him. We entered his father's office to talk freely. It was a very comfortable office with leather armchairs in crimson color.

'What would you like to drink Beni?' Taulant asked me.

'Apple juice please!' I answered to him.

'I called you because I wanted to talk with you about Gazi.' He went on.

'Ragarding what?' I got worried.

•　　•　　•　　•　　•

'We were playing basketball with my friends. Gazi was with us. After the match we went to drink something because we dehydrated while playing and were thirsty. We at the coffee bar in Fidan's neighborhood. Albion took beer while Gazi was in the restroom. When Gazi came back and saw the beer, he asked:

'Who ordered this?'

'I ordered it.' Albion answered to him.

'Are you an unbeliever? How dare you drink beer? Do you know that you will end up in Hell if you go on like that? Do you know that Allah forbid us to drink alcohol? Don't you fear Allah?' Gazi looked very angry.

'First of all, don't offend me! I haven't killed anyone to talk me like that. Besides, we used to drink beers together. Did you forget about that?' Albion was really surprised and hurt.

'What's up with you, Gazi? Calm down! We used to drink beer together and you enjoyed too. Did you forget that?' I had to interfere because I couldn't bear his behavior. 'We understand that Islam forbid it but can't force people to do things against their will. We alcohol is harmful. Even the science says so but we can't advise people in the rude way you just did. It is you psychotic behavior that instigates the opposite reaction.'

'Who are you calling psychotic?' Gazi got angrier.

In fact this word slipped off my tongue but it was too late.

'I am sorry!' I tried to apologize.

'I don't need your apology. You take sides of a sinner who drinks alcohol. You are as identically as him, a sinner. You will see who I am. You deserve to die from my hands.' He stood up and stormed against me.

Faruk prevented him from punching me. You know I have never had any problems with anyone in my life, Beni.

'O my God, with that boy! He is not the same since he has gone to Imam Beka's preaching.' I explained to Taulant.

'Who is Imam Beka, a cousin of Gazi?' Taulant asked surprised.

'No he is a manipulator, an ignorant, a demagogue, who is leading many young boys and men astray. He finished his studies about theology in seven years instead of four years.' I explained to him.

'What am I supposed to do with Gazi?' He answered me.

'Try to avoid him as much as possible. I will talk to him. Don't worry!' But I myself was worried.

'How do the Police let this Imam instigate people like that?' Taulant insisted.

'Maybe they know about him and they are going to do something about him.' I guessed.

'What do you think? Should I denounce Gazi to the Police?' Taulant asked me.

Maybe he was right. That would prevent Gazi from doing any harm to his friends, family and society, especially to himself. Anyway I answered Taulant:

'No, don't denounce him! I will talk to him. He must give up these stupidities once forever, for our sake, especially for his sake.' I tried to calm Taulant down.

I was scared about Gazi. After all he was my best friend. And indeed he was a goodhearted boy. He was so helpful to Adnan, being like a real brother to him. And he was there for us whenever we needed him. I didn't want him to end up in a prison cell like a criminal.

'Ok I will not denounce him.' Taulant said in the end.

Part]]

Chapter 1

It felt like I was flying. The problem was until he caught me back in the air. It felt like my bowls were moving inside my belly. My father used to throw me in the air and catch me up when he came back from work or when we turned back together with my mother from my uncle's. My father was a bus driver. He had a habit. While arriving home he used to greet my mother first and then calling me. I ran at him like a blowing wind. As far as I can remember, I was four or five years old at the time. Being an only child then, I felt jealous because my mother came first in his attention. He loved and respected her so much. In exchange, my mother behaved with him so correctly. I never saw them to argue. My father passed away when I was seven years old, but I remember my parents only enjoying their time together. My mother used to call my father "my sweetheart," whereas my father called her "my orchidea."

'My orchidea, didn't you have time to cook for today?' He used to say to mother. 'Let's go to your favorite restaurant to eat fish.'

As I remember we used to eat out often. When it was good weather, we walked, maybe perhaps my father used to sit long hours on the bus seat. The itinerary was a bit stretched, but he held me in his arms until we reached the restaurant on the lake shore. Sometimes I wanted to walk, ending up in a completion with my father who reached the destination first. He used to ply with me always. He never got tired of fulfilling my desires and my mother's.

That night we came back from the restaurant a bit sad, because my father had a very bad headache. It had appeared recently to him becoming more and more unbearable. He put his head on my mother's lap so she could massage him. I put my head on his breast to comfort him.

Chapter 2

My mother entered her parents' home where she left me because she went with my father at the hospital.

'What's the result?' My grandmother Xijë asked my mother anxiously.

Usually my mother was a symbol of the strong woman. But in this case, although she was trying to hide her worries, her face betrayed her. Something had gone seriously wrong. You could understand it from her face expression.

'God guard him and give him patience, mother!' My mother said to my granny Xijë.

My grandmother kept looking at my mother speechless.

'We must be strong.' My mother went on to comfort her, at the same time, trying to comfort herself.

'What are the test results?' My grandmother wanted to know the truth.

'Let me sit first!' And she threw herself on the sofa helpless. 'Brain tumor. My husband has brain tumor.'

Her voice began to tremble. She was almost crying. She went to the bathroom. She didn't want her mother see her suffer that much because her mother had a weak health too.

'God help you all!' Granny Xijë said worried.

I was already six years old at the time and Besa was just born. My granny kept sighing. I kept looking at her in a maze. When she became aware of that she told me to go out and play football. I went out but as there were no other children in the yard I began to through my ball against the wall of my granny's house.

When we arrived home, my father was folding a piece of white paper. He put it in his pocket. He greeted us but didn't hold me up as usual. However he put on the fool and tickled me and hugged me dearly. My mother looked at us sadly and thoughtfully. She just knew that her sweetheart had his days shortened.

Besa, four months old was sleeping on the sofa. My father wanted to hug her too but withdrew immediately because he didn't want to wake her up. But my mother urged him:

'Never mind, she slept enough for now.'

My father took baby Besa in his arms and kissed her with a fatherly tenderness, mixed with sadness. In the meantime, he kept me near him. Then he left Besa and me and sat down to talk with my mother. He was trying to comfort her, but a tear drop her face.

'Does your head ache?' She asked my father.

'Yes badly.' He answered to her.

She took him by his head and put it over her lap. She thought her massage would relieve him somehow of his unbearable headache. I was lying down and looking at my mother massaging my father's head while she was crying silently. She thought I was sleeping. My mother wasn't yet thirty four years old when my father died.

Chapter 3

I visited my father every day at the hospital. His headache had become unbearable. His tumor had advanced. When his headache was really unbearable he closed his eyes and tightened his jaws. My mother who was sitting by his bed kept massaging his head but in vain. My mother kept crying unceasingly since the day the test results went out.

In the meantime, I doctor entered the room hospital where my father was receiving treatment. My mother stood up and asked him about my father's health:

'We must be strong and be prepared for everything possible. Anyway miracles can happen.' He said to my mother in an effort to reassure her.

He knew very well my father's health condition was dramatic. However he tried to explain to my mother in an implicit way that my father was in his last days. He could understand my mother was an intelligent woman. While my mother was talking to the doctor, my father opened his eyes and made me a sign with his right index finger to go near him.

I stood up from my chair and obeyed to him. He felt it was his last time to see me. He was crying. He was not ashamed anymore to hide his tears. He knew he couldn't hold me anymore in his arms, he couldn't compete with me in running to let me win always. I was looking at my father crying and promised myself that if my father became better I would let him win the competition. Suddenly I stood up and storm onto him kissing him on his forefront, on his wet eyes and face. It was like I saying to him:

'You aren't going anywhere. I won't let you go anywhere.'

My mother came near us and kissed me on my head. Then she wiped my father's face and eyes. She kissed him in his forehead with utmost love. A knock in the door and my granny entered. I turned in my chair, while my mother took granny Xijë aside to talk in private.

Chapter 4

We stayed together with Besa at our uncle's house. Nanny Xijë stayed with us all the time. We slept at her room together with her. My mother stayed at the hospital all the time. My father's health deteriorated.

I woke up in the morning and was going to the bathroom when I noticed a strange mood in my uncle's house. My granny and my cousin Albina were talking to each-other in a strange way. My granny took me with her. We were going to my house for the first time after a few days I was staying at my granny's, while Albina had to take care of Besa.

When we entered into our front yard I felt like my father was waiting me at the door and I almost run to reach him, but no... My aunt took me in her arms and hugged me crying. I couldn't understand much. My mother had put a headscarf too.

'Beni, my dearest son, your father left us. You must become a strong boy to make your father proud in Heaven until we meet him again there.' She said to me.

She had no more tears in her eyes. It seemed that she found strength in her sadness and her sorrow. Her strength comforted me and I felt like my father had gone somewhere and could come back one day:

'Who am I supposed to play football with and run until I meet him again?' I asked her.

'You will play with me.' She went on to comfort me. 'Only you have to be patient and wait a week until our guests leave.'

Chapter 5

I was in sixth grade while looking in a drawer for a birth certificate I found a letter that was handwritten. It raised my interest because with "my dearest orchidea." That urged me to read it further. Anyway, I still had no idea what the word "orchidea" meant. I locked myself in my room and read:

My dearest orchidea,

I never thought we would be separated so early. But now that I have to accept my departure I need to tell some things that I preserve deep inside me. I wanted you to read this letter in front of me so I can see its effect in your eyes. This would give me strength to face my affliction. However I am suppressing my egoism and spare you from this suffering.

First of all I want to tell you that you are the most worthy and the dearest person to me, after my mother and my father that I loved them so much. I am thankful to the Creator that crossed our fates. I can't imagine what my life would have been without you, your unlimited love, your dedication and devotion toward me and our children, without your patience in abundance like the ocean. You were my best adviser and guided me to the best solution even when I saw no solution at all. You supported me even when me decision-making didn't match with our actual situation, and all this because you sensed my passion and you didn't want to see me sad. I appreciate your support now more than ever. I know that now I am in a helpless situation. You can't do anything about it. You did more than enough.

Since the day we took the test results every second of my life has become highly precious. Since that moment I understood how precious my life was. It wasn't easy for me. The end didn't mean closing my eyes forever. That meant leaving you and our two creatures here and going somewhere alone. You hide your tears from my, but I felt them. Your comforting massage lessened my pain and my suffering, but your tears stung my heart. I am telling you, I cried too. A tear is symbol of mercy. There is no shame to cry. We must face the trials that God has thrown upon us otherwise He would be angry with us. He knows best.

My dearest orchidea, you know that to me orchidea is the most beautiful flower in the world, and you were the most beautiful girl in the world to me. I know you are the best mother for our children however I want to confide you our children as a father not because I don't trust you. Try to play with Beni the plays I used to play so you can fill in somehow the gap that I am creating. Regarding Besa, ask her for my forgiveness I went away too early from her life. And help her not to feel the gap that I left behind.

My dearest orchidea, I know I am leaving you in a difficult situation. I know that now on you are going to be a mother and a father to our children. I know sometime you will feel vulnerable, but I am pretty sure that will bear the burden. You are a strong and an intelligent woman. It will come moments when you will feel powerless. In these moments please rely on your Creator and remember the happy years we went through together. I am sure you will find your strength there. And please forgive for every wrongdoing! I ask you for your "halal." You know the importance of "halal" in our religion. And another thing, don't be angry with God for taking me way from you, but always that you, me and the children will meet in Paradise!

With the utmost love and sufferance, your sweetheart!

The letter made me very sad. There I rediscovered his great love for us. I was too young when my father died but I remembered him quite well. In fact my mother followed his will correctly and more than that. Besa and I never bowed our head. Our needs were always fulfilled although the absence of our father was felt deeply.

Part III

Chapter 1

Five months later: One day I was watching a film at home suggested by Blerim, my classmate. It was about 23:00 hours. Suddenly I heard my phone ringing. It was a private number. I was curious to know who it was. When I heard a voice:

'Hello, Beni! How are you my friend?'

'I am fine thank you! Sorry but I don't know you.' I was very surprised.

'Don't you remember me? I am Fatlum.' He answered to me.

It's been five to six months since I hadn't heard from him. Besides, I had met him two or three times. I had no reason to remember him. After two or three seconds I recalled him. Then I cleared my voice and asked him surprised:

'Are you Fatlum, Gazi's friend?'

'Yes it's me.' He answered to me.

To tell the truth I didn't like the fact that he called me after all the things that had happened. However I was polite with him.

'Can we meet for a coffee?' He asked me.

Of course I didn't want to mingle with such a person especially after his acts and his imprisonment but I was to curious why he was inviting me and I accepted his invitation:

'Ok we can meet.'

We met after some minutes. He had changed completely. I was surprised by his good behavior, by his quiet and polite way of speaking. He said to me:

'Beni I guess you know the reason why I was imprisoned. Now I feel very ashamed for what I did.'

'Yes I know. I can understand you.' I didn't know what to say exactly.

'At the beginning I thought my act was going to be rewarded by God with Jannah. The first days in prison I entered into arguments with the inmates that opposed my opinions. After two months or so I went to another cell with two inmates, Fatbardh and Driton. Driton had a small beard. I considered Fatbardh a sinner, because he had shaved his beard. At the beginning I didn't consider him at all to talk to him let alone to respect him. Fatbardh was in jail for robbery, but Driton was there for no reason, according to him, at least. I got surprised. How do you get in jail for no reason at all. Driton tried to explain me the truth:

'I helped the drug addicted in my own house. I assisted them to leave the drugs and I succeeded somehow, but one day the Police knocked at my door and arrested me for being 'a danger to national security.' I got stunned. How was it possible that I was only working and I was even preparing to study my PhD in Islamic Sciences. I was too busy to be a danger for our national security. They took me with them and told me that they suspected I instigated the youth to go to war to Arab Countries. They accused me for meeting Imam Beka and collaborating with him. It's true we studied together at the same school but I was always against his ideology. It is true I met him a few times but I did that to advise him to give up that harmful ideology. I felt sorry for the youth that followed him. He guided the vulnerable youth astray.'

Fatlum went on:

'When I heard him speaking about Imam Beka like that I got really angry and I told him to shave his beard, because he didn't deserve it. Imam Driton tried to calm me down. He said that we would explain everything later. Regarding the beard, he told me that it was the Prophet's tradition, not obligatory and didn't make a man more or less religious. If you fill your head with useful knowledge, that makes you a pious person whereas the opposite makes you dangerous for the society. He spoke with a soft voice. He was so polite that I began to trust him. He was sentenced five years and a half. That was too unfair. You do good and you are rewarded with prison. But Driton was quiet. He had faith that his lawyer would solve everything positively. And indeed he was freed however after three months staying there. He advised me a lot during the time he was there. Thanks to him I went out of there transformed. Now he is the only person I seek advice to for religious issues. He has taught to do good in this world because I am accountable for it in front of God in the Day of Judgment. I have the best impressions from him. That's why I called you today Beni. Because you have self-control, you are not like Gazi, who loses his temper easily. I wanted to tell you that there is no better man than Imam Driton and that there is no worse man than Imam Beka. When I went to meet Gazi he didn't agree to turn away from Imam Beka and called me a deserter.'

Chapter 2

I am stunned Adnan. Gimi you can't imagine how much that boy has changed. He was repented deeply for the time he had lost with those extremists. He said that as he understood the truth now he wanted to contribute in the prevention of the youth falling prey to the clutches of those who your religion for their own interests. Agim and Adnan were delighted by my words about Fatlum. In the meantime, I felt someone's absence.

'It's been a week I haven't heard from him.' Agim said.

'Have you seen him Adnan?' I asked Adnan.

'I haven't seen him and I haven't heard of him ever since.' Adnan answered to me.

When we arrived at Gazi's home, aunt Bukuria told us that he had left. We were very happy with the news, but Adnan wasn't so happy, because Gazi was very helpful to him and in this way Adnan had lost a helping hand.

'When did he travel?' I asked aunt Bukuria.

'He left before a week. Didn't he tell you?' She told us.

'Jo he cut communication with us.' I felt guilty.

'I am sorry about that.' It seemed that she didn't know what had happened between us.

'No problem aunt Bukuria. The most important thing is that Gazi is going to enroll in that prestigious university. Maybe he didn't want to tell anyone until everything is for sure.' I tried to soften the situation.

'Did he call you?' Agim asked her.

'Yes as soon as he arrived there. He told me he was fine and gave me a phone number to call him whenever I wanted. He told me not to worry because he was waiting to follow the procedures of enrollment in the university.' Aunt Bukuria explained to us.

'Turkey has a very good education system.' Adnan said in the end.

'Thank you for coming. When I saw you at the door I felt like Gazi was back. I am happy he wants to open an opportunity for his life but I miss him. What can I do? I am a mother.' She said to us.

'Yes we can understand you. We know very well about your sacrifices to keep your family.' We replied to her.

'He is a very sensitive boy. Once I forget to knock at his door and found him sobbing and crying with his head in his hands sitting at his room table. I approached him I hugged him and asked about what had happened. He told me that he kept thinking about Beni, that he might have fallen victim of that terrorist attack in Brussels and he was terrified with the idea. It might have been a catastrophe even if he remained on wheelchair. Adnan was enough for him. He kept worry about you as you were his own brothers.' And she raised her hands toward the heaven, praying: 'O God, destroy those criminals that do harm in the name of religion!'

We were listening to her almost crying.

After a while she calmed down and we said to her that we appreciated Gazi very much and especially what he had done for Adnan. We hoped he enrolled the university and open his way to a worthy life. Aunt Bukuria thanked us:

'I am very happy I saw you. Thank you so much for coming! Come more often! When I see you it is like Gazi is here.' However she couldn't hide her sadness that her son was far away.

Chapter 3

It was a wonderful sunny day. I called Agim, Adnan and Fatlum to go out for a picnic at the park. We took a blanket and food and drink with us. It was the time of enrollment in the university. We need to share our views about our higher education. And we didn't cease to talk about how to help the youth not to be infested by the terrorist ideology while in country there were people who induce our youth to go to wars far away geographically and politically from us.

Agim told us that two days ago he heard about a boy from our city that became a suicide bomber in a city in Irak. He had been in his twenties. Fatlum had been schoolmate with his brother. Fatlum told us they were a very poor family. There were a number of young men and men from our country who joined terrorist organizations in conflict regions. They came mostly from families with economic or social problems. People like Imam Beka profited from their life conditions to guide them astray and exploit them for their dark interests.

In the meantime, Fatlum told us to meet with Imam Driton so we could learn from him and more strong minded and more successful regarding our mission for restoring peace and harmony in our community. Fatlum spoke very well about Driton:

'You know he is very quiet and a man of integrity. He is a man of knowledge and wisdom. He is encyclopedic. He has a way of explaining things that persuade the most stubborn and ignorant person. It is his behavior that made me change mind about many things and made me a better person.'

'In which mosque does he preach?' I asked Fatlum.

'He is going to London for his PhD so he isn't engaged anywhere for the moment. He has big plans for the future. He told me that after turning back from England he will open a social center for helping and rehabilitating the young men and men with drug, alcohol, gambling problems as well as social and family problems.' He answered to me.

'Well done to him. These are the real duties an Imam must have. Imagine Imam Driton's ambitions comparing to Imam of the White Mosque. We went once for the evening prayer and we told him we had a project about preventing the extremist ideology among the youth but he wasn't interested at all. He stayd with us just a few minutes for courtesy and went away. When we asked him to meet another time he said us that he was extremely busy. Thus I could understand why Muslims are in such big troubles. This Imam isn't worried about Muslim youth and the problems related. He just goes to Funeral dinners, and weddings. As long as the most of Imams waste their time thinking about financial and material profits with individual social activities they have no time to worry about the issues that trouble our youth and our youth will suffer further because of their negligence. If there were more Imams like Imam Driton who put the general interest over theirs and never aim at material profits our Muslim community would way much better. We need to meet him as soon as possible.' I told Fatlum in the end.

'Ok Beni I will tell him.' He was very willing to meet us with him.

Each of us made a plan what to talk with him about. I wanted to ask him about the war in Islam and its conditions. In these difficult time some people have given themselves to declare war to anyone who doesn't comply with their ideology. They speak in the name of Islam even if they have read only four or five books about Islam all in all. I needed to discuss this topic eagerly because this issue had fallen in the wrong hands. We might cooperate with Imam Driton in a positive and fruitful direction.

Chapter 4

We didn't want to bother him in his house, but Fatlum insisted that he wanted us to visit him exactly in his house and nowhere else. I felt immediately the difference to elsewhere. He welcomed us with a warm smile and greeted us cordially:

'Salam Alaykum! Feel at your home!'

After our presentation he began the conversation:

'I will be very sad if you are shy or hesitate to make any question or any comment possible.' He made us to feel at ease.

Fatlum was right. Only a person with broad knowledge and open minded accepts any opinion possible and isn't afraid of other people thoughts. The fact that he was open with us meant that he had good intentions. Not like Imam Beka who lost his temper every time I asked him. Imam Beka and his group were hermetic because they had something to hide. They wanted you only to hear them. They offended you if you asked them questions. Imam Driton had nothing to hide so he was open to any question.

'Fatlum have spoken very well about you and we can see with our own eyes he was right.' I started first. You seem a very understandable person. I am telling this to you because I have known rude people who consider themselves Imams but have nothing to do with Islam. To my surprise I couldn't talk to them freely let alone ask important questions to them.' I tried to explain to him.

'It is a shame when you have questions but you are too shy to ask or you hesitate. On the other hand it is a sign of arrogance and narrow minded or worse ignorance when someone accountable isn't willing to answer. The situation might become tricky or even dangerous.' And he went on. 'It is not a shame not to know but not to ask. The first verse in the Holy Quran is "Read!" that means "learn, explore for the truth and enquire about life." Asking questions is the next step toward mastering knowledge. In the human mind happens a process with some phases: having curiosity, asking questions, reading, meditating and we use that information for useful purposes to please God.'

'Honorable Imam Driton, we live in difficult times when people kill in the name of the religion. How would you explain the real concept of Jihad in Islam?' I went to my point.

'All the wrongdoings and the afflictions to the Muslims are happening because the matters regarding Islam have fallen in the hands of the incompetents.' Imam Driton tried to explain. 'The today's world is filled with injustice. The ignorant is giving competence for knowledge. Imagine something! Today executions are sentenced and wars are proclaimed by people who have no competences in religious matters.'

'Ok but who is competent for such matters and what are the conditions to proclaim a war in Islam? Please if you can explain it because we need to be clear about this matter!' I was seriously interested and he was really trying to help us.

'My dear brothers in faith, the wars have accompanied the humanity since its creation on earth. When you say "war" you think about all the atrocities that a merciless human being can commit. Despite the advancing of technology and communication between nations unfortunately the war has still remained a bitter phenomenon and of course there are inciters of wars. Islam as an all-embracing religion having its answers for every aspect of life especially such an important matter as war has its own rules and regulations regarding war. First of all the Academics and the Imams of a Muslim country must qualify a war condition when its security, and freedom and honor, and religious principles are threatened to specify a real threat and a real enemy in order to proclaim war against that enemy. An individual or a specified group has no right to proclaim war against a qualified enemy by them in the name of a specified nation. It is categorically forbidden in Islam. Our Prophet has taught us to depend on the Holly Quran and on his Tradition regarding any matter in Islam and to ask actual competent people in religious, political and military field. Muslim community must remain in a defensive position and fight back only when Muslim people are attacked. This is the first principle of war in Islam. In the Holly Quran the Omnipotent commands us: "And fight in Allah's path and overdue it..." Through this verse we can see that Islam doesn't instigate war, it even doesn't attempt to bring destabilization, however defense and self-defense are important especially moral and integrity of Islam are being violated: ...And when they attack you, counter attack them... So Islam evaluates peace highly and encourages the interfaith and interracial understanding. However Islam regulates the conditions of a war situation in the utmost right way.

'Don't they fear God while speaking in His name?' I still insisted.

'Beni I am very delighted to have met you. Your prospective seems high. Regarding the second condition about war, the main reason of war should be restoring peace and justice for the sake of their God. Every time that certain groups or individuals instigate was for other interests than those regarding principles of Islam, like in the case of terrorist organizations this is totally against Islam and its principles, since the Battle of Badr between Muslims and non Muslims. Thus civil war, ethnic cleansing, racial cleansing, ideological war are against the principles of Islam. If Muslims distance themselves from terrorist organizations that operate wrongly in the name of Islam they will do a great favor to Islam and the Muslim community, no matter what their enemies have planned against them.' Imam Driton was fairly clear.

We remained speechless. Then Fatlum asked him impatiently:

'What is the third rule, Imam Driton?'

Imam Driton smiled and went on:

'The third rule is war but not massacre and genocide. A Muslim must take into account that even in frontal battles he must avoid as much as possible crime and genocide against his enemy and this must happen in accordance with the teachings of the Holy Quran. The killing of innocent people, women, children and elderly is categorically forbidden in Islam. The massacres and the genocides committed by others against dead people or alive mustn't be an example to take by Muslims. It isn't justified in Islam, by no means. On the contrary, Islam condemns it strongly. Those people who behead and mutilate people in public and transfigure cadavers don't belong to Islam. They don't represent the Islamic teachings. On the contrary, they will be highly accountable for their ill doings in the Day of Judgment.' Imam Driton concluded.

'So according to you the actual wars and terrorist attacks have nothing to do with Islam? Are you saying that, on the contrary, the wrong doers will be punished severely by God about that?' I went on asking.

'This will happen without no doubt, Beni. This is confirmed by the Holy Quran and the Prophetic tradition. When we speak about "qatl" and "qatil" we mean "killing" in war conditions, killing the eminent enemy who's attacking us in order to kill us, not innocent civilians. Thus "war" is a "fight between two armies," not attacking schools, hospitals, neighborhoods, airports, shopping centers, bus and train terminals. We must study thoroughly and rationally the Islamic teachings about war, and respect and follow them correctly. This means that we must engage in a fair war, and not commit massacres and genocide. Prophet Muhammad has categorically forbidden us from the mutilation of a human being without any reason, especially cutting someone's ears, nose etc. He even ordered Muslims not to curse the dead enemies because that would offend their relatives.' I was amazed by his exhaustive explanation.

Then Imam Driton went into the kitchen to prepare us some coffee and we went on discussing about what he just had explained to us. Agim said a prayer with loud voice:

'O God, may you increase the number of Imams like Imam Driton!' Then he turned talked to us. 'Don't you think that only if the twenty per cent of Imams in the world were men of high integrity and masters of knowledge like Imam Driton the Islamic world would be much better? I think the whole world would be a better place for all of us.'

When Imam Driton came back into the sitting room with a big tray in his hands where he had put a coffee pot with four cups on it, I began again:

'What about jihad as a concept or was that all?'

'Do you think that the concept of jihad and that of the war in general is the same thing?'

'Yes, I was thinking so. To tell the truth I think that there is a slight difference between jihad and the war in general.' I presented him my perception about the two concepts.

'My dear brother Beni, I have to contradict you. The difference between jihad and war in general is so big that I am surprised how they even make a comparison between them. They are two opposite things. My dear brothers, jihad must be understood as an endeavor to pass form a bad condition to a good one. It means improvement of deeds. There is only one connection between jihad and the war in general: the wars in general are filled with irrational actions, killings, rapes, violence, all kinds of monstrous tortures, massacres against the one owns family members, and jihad must be the factor to guarantee the prevention of such atrocities, and no revenge in case they suffered such atrocities. This is where jihad is implemented. Jihad means striving, struggling with best purposes. Jihad must be implemented in terms of respecting the principles of a fair war, in an effort to endure and leave the judgment to the Supreme Judge if your beloved ones suffered massacres and genocide. Today some people do the opposite of jihad in the name of jihad. After returning from the Battle of Badr triumphant, Prophet Muhammad (p.b.u.h) told to his friends:

'You have just returned from the smaller jihad to the bigger jihad.'

Surprised by his words, they asked him:

'What is a bigger jihad if it isn't going to war against the enemy?'

'Bigger jihad is the struggle against the negative soul.' Driton quoted Prophet Muhammad saying.

Agim went on with questions:

'What does it make those young men and men to commit extremely violent acts with the illusion that they are ordered by Islam?'

'Very smart question.' And he went on with his brilliant interpretation: 'Agim my dearest brother, there are some factors that make those young men and men act so. Religious ignorance is the first component. Acting without knowledge is craziness. The ignorant is unable to withstand other people's provocations. He can easily go crazy and can be proud of his crazy acts, being sure he is reacting conform religious rules and regulations. The ignorant looses easily his temper thus the manipulators can manipulate him. The emotional conditions in a person are the second component. In that person reason and emotion are disconnected. Such a person can turn into a heartless beast, because they are led by their instincts like animals. Horatio Walpole, a politician and a man of knowledge said: *Life is a tragedy for those who feel and a comedy for those who think.* Emotional people fall easily prey of the cheaters and manipulators.'

'O brothers, once I was one of those.' Fatlum interfered half in jest. Then he went on thoughtfully:

'For a certain period of time I acted without thinking. Maybe it's my good luck that I bit that poor boy that day in the mosque and then to meet Imam Driton in prison. Maybe the worst would have happened to me: I would have killed someone or I would have committed a suicide attack.'

'Honorable Imam please could you tell us something about the manipulators that manipulate n the name of religion to lead the youth astray?' I asked him.

'In a target group where the ignorant people rule and in the meantime they can't control their emotions and their temper, they can easily be provoked by certain situations and make wrong decisions. The manipulators play a key role in this case. It is a clear fact that the difference between those who commit terrorist acts and the comrades of Prophet Mohammed is extreme. Today are shown videos about so called Islamists who kill innocent people, meanwhile the first cousin of Prophet Mohammad, Ali (G.b.p.h.) reacted very wisely when facing one of his enemies and threw him down. His enemy spit him on his noble face but Ali didn't kill him although he could kill him easily. Some of his friends reproved him about that but Ali told them that when his enemy spit on him Ali himself was so angry about that that he could have killed him and be accountable in front of God about killing someone out of wrath and not out of fighting in the name of God.' Thus Imam Driton gave us a very useful illustration.

'Honorable Imam Driton may I answer you another question? How is it possible that you and Imam Beka followed the same studies in an Arab country and you even studied at the same university but you have opposite opinions about the same religion.' I went on.

'Good question Beni. It is true that we have studied at the same university, but the difference in our opinions consists in that Beka wants to establish an Arab mentality about religion and life in our country meanwhile I try to adapt my teachings to the mentality of our country. He thinks that everything Arabs do is Islamic. He doesn't accept the fact that Arabic lifestyle is about traditional but not religious lifestyle. So why should we bring Arab traditions to our country?' Imam Driton was being very clear.

'How is it possible that you understand and accept that Islam must adapt to our traditions and our lifestyle bu Imam Beka and those who share the same ideas with him don't accept that?' I insisted.

'The point is that Imam Beka and people like him follow a certain ideology and read certain authors according to them authoritative authors but don't read the real authoritative authors. A person can't open his mind if he doesn't consider all the perspectives. Thus these individuals don't study contemporary authors. They are left back in time. They don't get actual information. They follow a selective source of information. This blocks the road to the true knowledge creating a huge between us and them tearing us apart.' While saying these words Imam Driton looked sad.

'You are saying that all this happens because they follow a certain stream of religious ideology and they read certain authors?' I asked him surprised.

'Exactly, Beni. It is normal to be against something that you are alien to. Their opinions are based on deficient studies. That's why they are dangerous for our society. Those people have completed their studies on Islamic Sciences and Islamic Jurisprudence and so on, but they are ignorant about religion because they study only one version of it and they are not able to make valid comparisons and deductions. You know the expression 'the lame doctor kills you, the lame Imam ruins your religion.' Imam Driton explained to me.

'How is it possible that on one side our religion orders us to respect our parents and on the other side I have heard complaints from the parents of those children who follow that stream? How is it possible that those individuals claim to be highly religious but don't respect their parents as Islam orders them?' I insisted.

'A Muslim who doesn't respect his parents is committing a big sin. They have learned a lame religion without order of rules and regulations. They give more importance to secondary and tertiary rather than to primary rules in Islam or they follow some rules cent per cent and neglect others. For example, they think if they pray everything is ok with them, they are cleaned up by all sins. In fact prayer is important in Islam, but its aim is not to make you unaccountable for anything. It is just to make you improve as a person. If the opposite happens, we need to know how we are praying, that is, the aim of our prayer. Many young men are manipulated by certain people claiming to be religious leaders. Those leaders speak only about praying five times a day and leave other issues that are important in Islam. Those ignorant so called Imams forget that prayer is one of six thousand rules and regulations in Islam. After all, what are we supposed to expect from those ignorant and manipulators? Maybe Fatlum can illustrate that because he passed through that circle.' Imam Driton went on.

Fatlum nodded his head:

'Yes, exactly. We used to talk about jihad and how to become a shaheed, and how a shaheed was rewarded, about the seventy two virgins who aawaited him in Jannah. In fact we used to hear only about how to die in the way of Allah.'

'My good boy Fatlum, you don't have to die like this in the way of Allah. My dearest brothers, these are the ways of the manipulators to send our youth astray. The start it with brainwashing by saying that this world is worthless and that you shouldn't waste your time with it. Then they tell them that there is a way to guarantee a better Afterlife. They repeat and stress the stories about the afterlife. According to them, there you can live the real life and be rewarded for your good deeds. God take revenge on those who manipulate our youth! They terrify them by saying that if they give priority to this life, they will be burn in Jahannam. They speak only about God's punishments and they forget to say that "My Mercy prevailed over My Wrath... And then they speak about Jannah and shaheed and his rewards in Jannah. Dear brothers, beware of that! Killing and war are two things that God hates. We must avoid them in all their forms possible unless they remain the last solution remained. If you take part in unjust wars and get killed with excuse that you are falling Shaheed, you will meet your God as a killer and you will be punished severely about that. Believe me, I pray for those young men and women who went abroad to fight in suspicious wars. Some of them commit terrorist acts thinking they are pleasing God, but no! They are completely wrong. Those criminals who sell themselves as religious leaders are sanding them to disgrace.' Imam Driton was more than clear.

'We have much work to do, Imam Driton. We need your help.' I said to him.

'Yes, Beni, we will try together to save them. I am very happy that there are still young men that want the best for our country and our society. I am in your disposal. You can call me whenever you need me.

And don't forget one thing: It is dangerous to tell them eye to eye that they are wrong so beware of them!'

'Ok.' We said.

We thanked him for his warm welcoming and for his brotherly words.

Chapter 5

We left his house with the best impressions about him. We headed to a coffee bar to talk about the possibilities to cooperate with the honorable Imam Driton. We needed more supporters. Besides, we knew the path we had chosen wasn't easy at all. Suddenly Fatlum talked us about a twenty two year old boy Burim who was about to be a suicide attacker but changed his mind in the last moments. He was from a village cross border. He is a fugitive because an arrest warrant is issued by the judge to arrest him. Agim and I felt sad with the fact that he had to go to prison although he repented. Agim said to us that boy must be taken into a rehab, and not detained, because that may influence negatively on members of extremist and radical groups who repent and change their minds. Also that boy would help the police with information about the operational strategy and the tactics of his extremist and radical group, thus giving a clear idea about extremist groups in general. I asked Fatlum to meet us with him. The point was that on one side he was hiding from his extremist group for being a deserter, and on the other side he was hiding from the police who was looking for him everywhere. Agim had another fear:

'If we meet him in secret, the police would think we are collaborating with him.'

When he heard Agim's words, Fatlum became hesitant:

'Maybe it is better to wait a bit until his situation calms down.'

But I insisted to meet him before he could be arrested:

'We can learn a lot from him. He can help us more than anyone else. We will not misuse our meeting with him. He must be aware about his contribution in preventing our youth from going astray.'

'We mustn't be scared. We knew since the beginning that this would be a difficult path to follow so I support Beni's idea.' Adnan confirmed.

Fatlum and Agim looked at each-other and nodded:

'We will meet him if Burim agrees.' He said.

Chapter 6

We needed to meet Burim first then call the conference. The meeting with him would help us specifying the topics to be presented at the conference. Then Fatlum called him:

'Salam Alaykum, my brother Burim! How are you? What's up? As I told you, my friends and I want to meet you. We have planned a conference due after ten days: 'Helping the youth become aware of the deviations in the name of religion.' So if it is possible tomorrow or after tomorrow, so we can make the conference more fruitful.'

The situation became tense. He might have changed his mind or he even might have become suspicious about us. Suddenly Fatlum covered his mobile phone with his left hand and asked us:

'When do you want to meet him, tomorrow or after tomorrow?'

We agreed to meet him the next day. Then Fatlum asked for our permission because his mother was recovered in the hospital to have a surgery. We volunteered to accompany him. We found her lying in her bed taking an intravenous fusion. Fatlum helped his mother to stay sit. He put a pillow over her back. His mother looked at me for a few seconds then she asked me:

'You must be Beni.'

'Exactly, how are you?' I asked her.

'Better, thank you! You aren't yet aware about the responsibility you are taking on your shoulders.' She told me.

I remained a bit surprised.

'Fatlum told me about you, and Agim and Adnan. He is amazed especially by your maturity and intelligence. Can you imagine how much grateful I am to you?' She said to me.

'To tell the truth I am a bit surprised by your words.' I was really surprised.

'Beni, come sit here, nearby me!' It was clear she was fond of me.

I sat on her right. She took me by my hand looking at me silently. When she began to talk I saw tears in her eyes. She breathed deeply with her nose and said:

'There is no more human deed than to save the youth from the extremist and radical mentality. You are engaging in such deed. Can you imagine how a youth's parents, grandparents, siblings, all his family feels when he falls prey to the clutches of some people who think of nothing else but destruction, slaughtering and bloodshed of innocent people? And can you imagine their happiness when their loved one gets away from the same devils with human image. I have passed this experience myself with Fatlum. My family and I were in big stress at the time because Fatlum became very arrogant. I don't intend neither to discredit nor to offend him in front of you, but I just want to tell you what happens in these cases so can be highly motivated to save those youth who are in danger.'

Fatlum had bowed his head wiping his tears touched by his mother's words and his sincere repentance:

'I don't get offended by your words my dearest mother. On the contrary I feel sincerely sorry for my wrongdoings in the past.'

He approached her to kiss her on her forefront. She tried to wipe his tears but the intravenous tube didn't let her. Then she went on:

'The most difficult moment was when he started to refuse eating the food I prepared to him, with the excuse that I was an unbeliever.'

She began to cry and she went on with a trembling voice:

'We didn't dare to speak to him. He had gone wild. We once tried to advise him to go away from that Imam Beka who broke the hearts of many mothers, God curse be upon him. He is a devil with the face of a human being. His father told him to beware of that man. We were ok that Fatlum want to practice Islam but we didn't want our son to follow that ignorant and manipulator. Fatlum got very angry when he heard his father speaking against that Imam Beka. He broke our heart by claiming that he respected him more than us. You will be accountable in front of God for that and he went out. It was our good luck he ended up in prison to meet there with Imam Driton. Now we are very happy that he stays with you instead of that cursed group. So don't stop helping those youth. Thus you will help their families too.

She motivated me with her words and warmed my heart. Agim and I wished her a soon recovery and were about to leave. When we reached the door she told me:

'God help you, restorers of peace!'

Chapter 7

The next day we met at seven o'clock in the morning. Fatlum's cousin came with his car. He offered to accompany us. We called Burim once again. We needed to be sure. He might have changed his mind. Burim had found shelter in a village across the border. We set off. We had a long itinerary ahead of us. However we had a nice ride. Fatlum's cousin, Faton, was a nice boy. He was surprisingly very humble. He might have been in his middle thirties. Like Fatlum's mother he told us some episodes from the time when Fatlum was following Imam Beka:

'They were worried because they had heard a lot about the doomed end that expected the youth manipulated by such people as Imam Beka. They were very scared their son might become a suicide attacker. Believe me! Only those who experienced themselves such extreme situations can understand it well.'

When we were arriving near the border a police patrol stopped us. I got very nervous. Many thoughts roamed through my mind. When I looked at Agim, he was all pale. Fatlum got scared too. The first thought was, maybe they were surveying us.

'Your license and registration documents please.' The police officer said to Faton.

Faton showed him his car license and the documents.

'Where are you headed to?' The police officer asked him.

'We are going for an excursion cross border.' Faton answered to him.

'Ok but you are driving as if though you have an emergency like you are going to a hospital or to a funeral. You have surpassed the speed limits.' The police officer was about to fine him, but Faton behaved so correctly that the police spared him with a rebuke: 'Be careful next time! Take back your documents and have a nice trip!'

Now on Faton was much more careful. We crossed border without any problem but we had another one hour and a half ride to the village where Burim was hiding. We stopped at a gas station. We could eat something the diner there and we had a coffee too.

When we arrived at the village we were amazed by the view. A river went by the wood with big trees. Its water was clear like crystal. The hills were welcoming us. We filled our lungs with pure air. God makes miracles. We felt like we were in Paradise on Earth. When we were about to go back into the car we saw a boy with a cow coming toward us. Agim asked him:

'Do you know someone called Burim? He is from cross border.'

'We have two Burims in our village.' The boy answered.

He was about twelve years old. He went on:

'We have another Burim. He is a guest in our village.'

'Is he a slim boy with dark hair wearing a beard?' Fatlum described him "our" Burim.

'Yes and all the villagers respect him. He is a very good boy.' It seemed that Burim was doing well there.

'Yes exactly. We are looking for him. Where can we find him?' Fatlum asked him again.

'Go straight then on your right there is a shop. Ask the shopkeeper. He will tell you where the house of Bacë Faik is. Burim is his guest.

When we arrived at the shop I asked a girl who was selling there, possibly the shopkeeper daughter. The house was nearby. Fatlum knocked at the door to the house. An old man appeared at the door. I was sure it was Bacë Faik.

'God blessed me with guests right now.' The old man said. 'Welcome my sons!'

'We are honored.' Fatlum said. 'Is this the house of Bacë Faik?'

'Yes, I am Faik.' He said.

'We are Burim's friends. We came here to meet him.' Fatlum went on.

'Come inside! I will tell him.'

The door was lower than a normal door so we had to bow our heads while going inside. But when we entered inside we saw the inner part of a high housetop with timbers, all layered on straw. On the timbers were pended every kind of tools, mainly agricultural. On our left there was a mini-tractor and on our right there was the door to a room. In fact it was the fireplace room. We waited there until Burim came.

'Salam Alaykum!' He greeted us.

'Wa Alaykum Salam.' We replied to him.

He welcomed us one by one and we sat down. Then he stood up again and hugged Fatlum:

'I missed you so much.'

Then Fatlum introduced us. The old man and Burim welcomed us again this time nodding.

'Where are you from?' The old man asked us opening a tobacco-box and he lit a cigarette.

It seemed he didn't know Burim's secrets.

'I am going out to work. In the countryside the work never ends.' He said but in fact he wanted to leave us alone with Burim so we could talk freely with each-other.

'What is your connection with this family?' Fatlum asked Burim.

'Long story.' And he began to tell us. 'My father was best friend with his only son. My father was a migrant in Italy when they met. His son had just come there and my father helped him. Then he married to an Italian woman. They had a daughter together but he died in a car accident. His Italian wife together with his daughter remained in Italy. Bacë Faik remained alone when his wife died too two years ago. Bacë Faik's brothers live nearby but he is a very proud person. He never disturbs them. He works more than us that are young in age. When I came here I told him I was in trouble with the Police. He didn't want to know anything about that. He just felt in debt with my father about helping his son in the past and wanted to help me. He thinks he can somehow pay off my father. Besides, he told me that I would be a good company to him, someone with whom he could talk to.' Then Burim changed topic. 'How are you, my brothers?'

'Ok thank God.' We answered.

'I am very happy you are here. As Fatlum may have told you, I have gone through a dangerous trial, but thank God I didn't do any harm, neither to others nor to myself. At least I will meet my God not as a killer of innocent people. I know the purpose of your visit so I will speak with you openly. I trust Fatlum so I trust you too. What we planned to do was extremely dangerous with catastrophic consequences. We planned to go to a Christian country with Muslim population. Our purpose was to cause as many victims as possible. My duty was to be suicide attacker in a subway station. My two other friends committed the attacks and were killed during those attacks. I guess you have heard about that tragedy where more than one hundred and fifty people were killed. I couldn't go only because I broke my leg two days before the attack but Imam Beka ordered the two others to proceed anyway. They told me they would use me when I recovered.' He said.

'Sorry to interrupt but how did you change your mind afterwards?' I asked him.

'I told you I broke my leg. The period of recovery helped me to clear my mind. When I became aware about what I had been going to do I repented deeply.' He answered.

'Is it only this or are there any other reasons?' I insisted.

'Of course there are other reasons too. I will explain it step by step.' He said.

'Can you tell us first of all how you ended up there and what made you feel like almost going to the extremity?' I wanted to know the root cause of those acts.

'Yes Beni I will tell you everything I know so you can help the youth not to fall prey of such manipulations.' He was trying to be helpful. 'At the beginning I wanted to be in the path of God. One Wednesday I asked Bekim, a boy in my neighborhood, about Islam. We used to gather at the oak tree where uncle Baki had put a table and some chairs. In the end he invited me to the mosque for the Friday prayer. When we went out of the mosque after the prayer it felt like I was flying. Since that day I used to go more often to the mosque. I made new friends there. We used to go to religious meetings as well as excursions. The first year I changed positively. My family members used to praise me for that. I began to visit my kinship regularly. I showed deep respect to them for God's sake. It was like that until we went to a camping organized by a "humanitarian" organization. The preacher was Imam Beka who had just finished his studies for Islamic Jurisprudence in an Arab country. When we finished our evening prayer he went on with his preaching until our last prayer. The main topics were "there is no other religion accepted by God than Islam", 'a Muslim is a brother for another Muslim." He taught us that a Muslim wasn't completely Muslim if he didn't help unconditionally another Muslim. His concept was fine but the way he preached was scary. He used to raise his voice and cry, while his behavior was a bit arrogant. He made us feel guilty about Muslims being persecuted around the world. He used to make his audience. He made me cry too although I couldn't understand the reason of all that pathetic behavior. He planted in our hearts the hatred for non-Muslims.'

'What about during the day?' I asked him again.

'We mainly did physical exercises. We played football, we went jogging. Ah, I almost forgot. There was a karate instructor who taught us self defense techniques after afternoon prayer. Then we had dinner and prayed the evening prayer. One evening, Imam Beka talked us about Jahannam. He advised us shouting and crying making the audience cry too. I wanted to ask him a question but he got angry and silenced me arrogantly. He told me not to have doubts about his words because he backed his words with the Holy Quran and the Prophetic Tradition.' I knew what Burim was talking about and said:

'Of course the manipulators and the wrongdoers are covering up their sinister purposes with the Quran and the Sunnah.'

'You are right Beni but at the time I thought Imam Beka was right. One day an Arab man came and addressed us a speech about Jannah and the rewards that await a Muslim there. He spoke especially about the seventy two virgins that God promised for a shaheed who entered in Jannah. He was a fat man, wearing a jalabyah - a manly tall dress - and a white prayer cap. He presented his speech and Imam Beka translated. When I think about it now, I can understand that all was premeditated. They wanted to brainwash us, especially the youngest ones and use us for their purposes. And they succeeded somehow. We used to become emotional easily. We cried during those meeting but we didn't know for sure if Imam Beka was right or not. After that camping we used to hate non-Muslims. They were God's enemies, thus our enemies. This ideology is spreading around the world. You can find people with such mentality everywhere. The most surprising and dangerous thing is the eloquence and the ability of individuals like Imam Beka to manipulate people. A young man that falls prey to their clutches acts like hypnotized. They deceit you and make you think the reality upside down. It is surprising that they can make you explode yourself in the air by promising you the Paradise and the seventy two Virgins misusing God's religion like they don't fear Him at all.' Burim explained to us.

'Do you remember Burim when Anas Talab told us at the mosque of the basement that if we loved someone we had to love him for God's sake and if we hated him we had to hate him also for God's sake.' Fatlum recalled.

'Yes of course I remember it. Maybe they didn't know or didn't want to give the right meaning of the saying by the Prophet. By this saying they divided people into two categories, into Muslims and non-Muslims, into beloved and hatred people and nothing in between. The non-Muslims were considered enemies even though they were decent people. They hated also the Muslims who didn't practice Islam. They called them deserters. They say that the enemies of Islam that is the non-Muslims and the deserters that is the Muslims who don't practice Islam must be eliminated and the world must be ruled only by Muslims who practice Islam. In fact their interpretation is lame and their ideology is dangerous hiding evil purposes. They take some parts of Islam and explain them according to their appetite. Unfortunately those young men knew little about Islam and those Imams with sinister purposes know this well. On the other hand, they didn't tolerate those who knew about religion. They offended them and didn't let them discuss about a certain issue or even ask questions. Some of those young men went away never to come back. Imam Beka didn't want around him young men with knowledge and conscience. He wanted robots to be manipulated and obey to him easily. Who didn't comply with their ideology they considered them deserters, cowards, enemies of Islam etc. This is an applied method.' He said.

Agim and I laughed. Burim and Faton looked at us surprised. Burim blushed. He seemed a bit offended. I immediately explained to him:

'Sorry but you reminded us our situation with Imam Beka. Listen, Burim! My family and I escaped a suicide attack at the Brussels airport so we suffered ourselves because of that sinister ideology. When I frequented Imam Beka's preaching I wanted to ask him but he would offend to shut my mouth. I am sure it is a practice he uses not to let his followers use their logic.'

'Exactly, Beni. They gather around themselves ignorant youth who trust them blindly and think emotionally and not reasonably. They are manipulated and commanded easily.' Burim supported my point.

His words made me think about Gazi, only that Gazi was spared somehow as he went to study abroad. Maybe there he will come to his senses. Suddenly Burim became aware that we had a long ride and maybe we were hungry.

Chapter 8

The food tasted so deliciously: casserole with rice and chicken, salad with tomatoes, onions and cucumber, natural yoghurt and cheese. Burim had cooked and prepared everything like a real chef. Bacë Faik smiled and said:

'Since Burim has come to my house I have gained ten kilograms. I am eating like e king. Burim is hardworking and diligent. He is a great boy.'

After dinner we had tea. Bacë Faik told us his version about his connections with Burim. Then he apologized another time and went out. It was clear he wanted to let us talk in peace. When we remained alone, Faton told Burim:

'Come on, tell us about their organization! We can't wait. It's like in a thriller movie.'

We laughed with Faton's comparison. It's true, looking it from a far prospective it was thrilling but in reality it was scary. Burim repented for what he had done in the past, sighed and bowed his head. Then he looked at Faton and said to Faton:

'I get goose-bumps when I think what I was going to do. Imagine, my brothers! I was going to enter a subway station in the busiest time of the day. We intended to attack as more people as possible. O my

God, forgive me please!' He raised his hands toward the sky with his eyes in tears.

Then he turned toward us:

'Sorry my dear brothers but do you understand in what degree I lowered myself? Can you imagine how many innocent non-Muslim people I would have killed? Let alone among them might have been Muslims too. And to think that even according to those radicals the killing of Muslims is categorically forbidden in Islam.' And Burim began to cry sadly.

The room became silent. We remained speechless. After he calmed down, Burim went on:

'I am sorry my brothers but I missed them so much, especially my mother. I don't know when I am going to see them again. I feel bad about them. When I came back for camping I was rude to them. I ruined my good relationship with them with my kinship with my friends because I was taught that they were not good Muslims, thus they were deserters. God forgive for my wrongdoings.' He breathed deeply and went on again: 'After we came back from camping we used to meet three times a week. Imam Beka went on with his preaching by proclaiming enemy all non-Muslims. He forbid us to read any other literature without his permission.'

'Couldn't you read at home, where Imam Beka couldn't see you?' Faton asked him.

We laughed with his naïve question. Burim answered him:

'The point is that his word was authoritarian. We obeyed him blindly. We even were willing to burn the books he forbade us to read. Also he said that a believer was distinguished from an unbeliever by the prayer he performed so we mustn't stay near those who didn't pray. According to him, they didn't deserve respect. We took his words so seriously that we caused problems in our families and with our friends with the excuse that they weren't good Muslims because they didn't pray five times a day as it was obligatory for a devote Muslim. Again, according to him, if they didn't pray they were considered unbelievers and they deserved to die from our hand. With their indoctrination and brainwashing they wanted to turn us against our parents, our brothers and sisters, and our best friends.'

Agim was looking at him stunned and said:

'You terrified us with your words. Was there any person left you considered a worthy individual?'

'No, it was only us. We created a closed circle. We were isolated totally from the outer world. We even didn't watch television anymore, except for religious TV programs. We used to take repeatedly information about revenge and terror against the "enemies" of Islam, Muslims and non-Muslims. This is their dangerous world where they live in.' He drank some water and went on:

'One evening when I went to pray the Isha' prayer as usual in the mosque of the basement I noticed a young man named Abu Hamza, but he wasn't Arab. His trousers went in the middle between his ankle and his knee, and he had a beard and a white cap on his head. He was sitting with Imam Beka and Anas Talab. After the prayer, they stayed together and Anas Talab invited me to join them. Abu Hamza spoke in Arabic and Imam Beka translated. He told me that he had heard about my bravery and strong will. Then he told that they had a plan for the sake of Muslims and that if I sacrificed myself I was promised seventy two virgins in Jannah and eternal life there. And I also could mediate for my family members in the Day of Judgment for them to enter them to Jannah. Then he went on telling me that I could be an excellent example of sacrifice in God's path for the Muslim youth and I would be honored as a shaheed in this life and Thereafter. I got goose-bumps and I accepted. In the end Anas Talab called for takbeer and the four of us said "Allah Aqbar!" Then Imam Beka said that he knew his group is ready to sacrifice himself for Thereafter. He called me a "lion." Abu Hamza confirmed him.' Burim got nervous again, then calmed down a bit and went on again: 'We went to train in the Alps near the border, together with Imam Beka and Abu Hamza. We stayed at the chalet of our group's member. We had to receive physical and mental training there. They addressed to us a motivating and emotional speech twice a day, two hours in the morning and two hours in the afternoon. At noon we had physical training. We were taught how to use a gun. We had to shoot first and kill as many people as possible then explode ourselves in the air. Each one of the three of us would carry two pistols and explosives wrapped around our bodies as much as not to be noticed. I trained on a regular basis until the fifth day I fractured my left ankle. It swelled and the pain became unbearable. Imam Beka and Abu Hamza became very nervous. That could sabotage their "mission." In the end they decided to go on with the attacks. They were committed by the two kamikazis left. There were many victims and the damage was huge. After the identification of the attackers they took information about me. I was told to hide somewhere. Two of my friends in the group were arrested but surprisingly not Imam Beka and Abu Hamza. I wandered ten days in the woods and in the fields until I could reach here.'

'How did you feel during the days of your training?' I asked him.

'Sometimes I was scared but when I reminded God's reward I was willing to do it. They kept us under emotional and mind control all the time.' He answered.

'What made you to change your mind about what you were going to do?' I went on with my questions.

'First of all, it helped me the accident. Then I began to think why Imam Beka didn't go themselves to commit the attacks and why all those who instigate others to commit suicide attacks don't go themselves to receive the utmost reward from God. And yet again I reminded the verse from the Holy Quran "Who kills an innocent person it is like he has killed all the humanity and who saves an innocent person it is like he has saved all the humanity." Then I asked myself what those people had done to us to kill them mercilessly. In the end I deducted that all that was done for destabilization and war against peace, harmony and religious tolerance in the world. That was the mere purpose of some sinister and ignorant people. They first isolated us and then indoctrinated and commanded us like robots. We became as blind as to believe that their words were holy. We couldn't think rationally anymore, just emotionally. And when you are ruled by emotional behavior you can become extremely dangerous.' Burim concluded his word.

Chapter 9

We went back home the same night. Burim helped us a lot with his story. He was aware that he was going to be arrested one day. He was even considering go himself to the Police. Anyway he was sorry that they were considering him a terrorist although he had repented.

At last we called the conference. We invited Imam Driton as a representative of the Islam, as well as a psychologist, a sociologist and an expert for security matters. Fatlum opened the ceremony:

'As one of the organizers of this conference and as one of those people who once had extremist and radical views I welcome you in this event entitled "Protecting the youth from the deviation in religion" with some lectures by personalities from various fields.'

After all the lecturers addressed their speeches finally it was the time for questions and free discussion. Imam Driton was asked:

'How is it possible that two Imams don't share the same points of view about Islam?'

'Islam has opened its doors to all people. Islam is like a vast ocean for us to swim into it. But some of us haven't learned well to swim and risk drowning if they aim deep waters. I mean maybe all people want to know about Islam or even become Imams but they must respect some rules and regulations. You mustn't take Islam emotionally but rationally. In some people violence and terror is planted deep in their personality and can manipulate others in the name of religion. On the other side a good Imam's intention is to introduce religion as a peaceful structure with main purpose the education of an individual with the best traits and virtues.' Imam Driton went on and on because the audience was eager to know the very the truth.

The conference was highly successful. We felt very motivated to organize other conferences and we discussed this with Imam Driton. He showed his highest willingness.

Chapter 10

One afternoon we were playing football and Agim, while trying to take the ball from me, pushed me and I fell. I hurt my knee severely but I didn't accept to go to the hospital. Instead I sat with Adnan by the football field. Adnan looked at me and said with a sad voice:

'How do you feel now that you became somehow invalid to play football? I never express that because I don't want to give the impression that I am jealous about you but I am deeply hurt.' I behaved like I didn't hear his words but he went on: 'Anyway I feel more relieved now that I can move with the wheelchair with battery.'

A tear drop rolled down my face and I said to him:

'Stop it Adnan! This is God's trial. He will reward you with the greatest reward with God's will.'

'This keeps me alive and strong Beni. I haven't lost hope in God's reward.' He replied to me.

In this very moment his mobile rang.

'Hello? Detective…? I have done nothing wrong. Ok but I can't go up to the third floor because I am disabled and I move on a wheelchair. Ok I will take the elevator then. See you tomorrow!' Adnan spoke on the phone.

'Who was that?' I was very curious and worried at the same time.

'It was detective Skënder. I don't know him but he told me to to go and meet him tomorrow morning at the Police Station 3.' He said me and asked me to go with him.

I reminded him that it was the same detective that I met some months ago. In the meantime, the match finished and Agim came toward me.

'How are you now, Beni? I am so sorry but I didn't mean.' He apologized again.

'I don't doubt about it. I am much better now. Don't worry. I will be fine.' I said to him.

The next day I accompanied Adnan to the Police Station. We entered Detective Skënder's office both and when I was about to leave them alone, detective Skënder said to me:

'I called him about Gazi. He is your friend too.' And he turned toward Adnan: 'We have information that Gazi called you a few days ago. Do you know what exactly is going on with him?' He asked us.

'Yes we know he went to study to Turkey. He went earlier to study Turkish. I am sure about that. We know Gazi well. He is a good boy.' I answered to him.

He looked at us with sad eyes. This was the second time he called us for Gazi. Then he changed topic:

'I heard you organized a great conference with a very interesting topic. It went viral. Congratulations for your initiative and good will. Go on like that! You are a big help to society and especially the youth. Well done!'

'It's our duty to protect the youth from manipulations and people with bad intentions.' I said to him.

He thanked us for our cooperation and we thanked him for his friendly and open behavior, and we left.

Chapter 11

My phone rang. I opened it.

'Beni, my sweetheart, how are you?' My blood flooded into my veins and I remained speechless for e few seconds, when she insisted: 'Hello, Beni? Are you listening to me?'

'Yes of course, my love.' I answered to her.

'How are you?' She was a bit worried.

'A little tired but I am ok.' I said to her.

'Listen, Beni! Grace invited us to her birthday.' She said.

'Ok have a nice time there. See you later!' And we hung up.

Then I called Agim and the others to meet at our favorite coffee bar. We were curious why detective Skënder was so interested about Gazi's activity. Me, Agim and Adnan didn't suspect but Fatlum seemed worried and suspicious although he didn't say anything. I invited the three of them at my house to watch the football match together. But there was one condition, to talk about football and nothing else. We decided to invite Imam Driton, too.

We sat in front of TV to watch the match. During the time break we zapped the channels. There was breaking news about a suicide attack in Turkey. Fatlum said instinctively:

'O God, let not be Gazi!'

We looked at him surprised. In that moment I told Imam Driton about detective Driton who called us twice about Gazi. Driton was very angry about the attack:

'Curse be upon them! What do they do? Why they do all this? Cursed terrorists send the youth to kill themselves and the others. Why don't they kill themselves instead…'

We were surprised. It was our first time to hear him curse. We saw tears in his eyes. He spoke to us:

'It's all Imams' fault. Instead of working with the youth to open their eyes against manipulators, killings, drugs, alcohol, gambling, suicide, they go to dinners, weddings, funerals and gatherings for material profits and think only to relax and entertain themselves…'

In the meantime, his phone rang. He talked to the other person and became pale. We looked at each-other speechless. We wanted to know what had happened exactly. Her hung up and turned toward us:

'Boys, I have a good news and a bad news. The good news is that they have arrested Imam Beka and two other individuals for recruiting young men and men for terrorist attacks.'

I was happy with the news. I looked at my friends. They were giggling. The happiest was Agim, because he feared Imam Beka and his group the most. Now we were waiting to hear the bad news. Imam Driton with his eyes looking down and a said voice told us:

'They say that there were three kamikazis, one from our city and two from Germany, of Moroccan origin.'

We bowed our heads. We didn't want for him to be a criminal and e suicide. We couldn't believe he had reached to that degree. The next day we went to Gazi's house to confirm our suspicions. When we reached Gazi's house we saw cars parked in front of his front yard. Agim, Gazi's cousin came to welcome us. He hugged me and burst into tears. I was trembling but didn't say anything. I asked him whispering:

'Was it Gazi?'

'Yes.' He answered sobbing.

I was shocked. I would have given everything only not to hear that confirmation. It was the same "yes" that confirmed my father's death.

'Yes it was him that entered the shopping center and exploded himself killing thirty six innocent people.' He explained.

Adnan was crying too:

'No, it's not possible.' He repeated, sobbing.

I entered the house and I saw Kujtim coming toward me:

'Gazi left us forever, Beni.'

His eyes and his face were red. He hugged me crying and sobbing. I could bear it. My heart was aching but I didn't want them to see eyes in my tears. I wanted to keep myself strong in front of them. I wanted to enter the room where aunt Bukuria was staying. She was crying and talking to a woman next to her. Kujtim called her:

'Mother!'

She turned toward the voice and when she saw me she came toward me. She hugged me crying and sobbing. She said:

'When I saw you, it was like Gazi came back.'

I couldn't bear it anymore. I burst into tears.

Through her tears she said:

'O God, curse on them! They took my son. They send him astray. They killed my son. O my God, what they did to me? They killed my son. They destroyed his dreams and my life. O God, curse on them!'

We were all crying.

'O my son, the light of my eyes, I send you there to come back with a university degree, not to end up in pieces in a foreign country, away from your mother. Your mother brought you up with great sacrifices.

Why did you that to me? How am I gone live now without you? Did you think about me, your brother, your family, your friends?' It was like she was talking to him in Heaven. 'O God, please take good care of him. Someone sent him astray. I know well my son. He wouldn't have done that. The devils made him do that.'

We sat on the balcony and began to talk. I felt guilty somehow. Maybe we could have prevented that, but Gazi had become very stubborn and he wouldn't listen to us anymore. My mistake was that I didn't insist to take him away from Imam Beka in the right time. Now I understood how much Gazi was manipulated by him. It was better for me to report Gazi to the Police. I was wrong not to tell detective Skënder about my suspicions. He might have stayed in jail for some time but that would have saved him from doing what he did. That would have saved him from the punishment in Hell – God know best - for killing innocent people although he was taught he would have entered into Paradise for that. That would have saved from the sufferings he caused to his family for his loss and for making them feeling guilty towards the family victims about their son. That would have saved us from losing our best friend. That made me once more firm in my mission.